COLLECTING

FLY

FISHING

CARL CAIATI

Alliance Publishing, Inc

ISBN 1-887110-11-9

Design by Cynthia Dunne

Alliance Books are available at special discounts for bulk
purchases for sales and promotions, premiums, fund
raising, or educational use.
For details, contact:

Alliance Publishing, Inc.
P. O. Box 080377
Brooklyn, New York 11208-0002

Distributed to the trade by National Book Network, Inc.

10 9 8 7 6 5 4 3 2 1

*To Marlin Greene, fledgling fisherman
and prospective collector.*

CONTENTS

ACKNOWLEDGMENTS

Fly fishing collectibles is a second time around book, almost a sequel to my first ad-encompassing fishing tackle collectible fishing manual. Again, I had the cooperation of some of the finest people around, collectors, manufacturers, and aficionados who gave freely of their time and expertise.

Tom Greene of Custom Rod and Gun graciously opened up his collection cases and his fine, keen, infinitely knowledgeable mind, providing me with a wealth of photographable material and useful information. A visit to Tom's shop is like a visit to the ultimate fishing museum. There is no end to what this man has collected in his life to date.

Carl Freeman Luckey, who has written the bible of collectible books, *Old Fishing Lures and Tackle*, was exceedingly gracious and helpful. Carl, a foremost expert, gave me some valued information over the phone and allowed me to use some old catalog material from his files. This is professional courtesy at its highest level.

Roxanne Coleman of Shakespeare always comes through with some good material for me, and we were able to integrate it into this book highlighting some vintage Shakespeare and Pflueger items.

I can't thank the American Museum of Fly Fishing enough. The curator of this Manchester, Vermont, historical archive, John Mathewson, also assisted greatly, allowing me to reproduce some material from their archives. A trip to the museum is a must for serious anglers who wish to digest some fishing history and at the same time study some really choice old fishing relics.

Terry Wilson assisted in the reproduction department by making the great prints that comprise the fine illustrative material, and Rodney Wood, killer on the computer keyboard, whacked out the endless copy sandwiched between the covers of this mini-manual.

Most of all, I want to pay homage to the kindred

spirits of anglers deceased who have so touched upon my life in the process of compiling my data. What an ethereal experience to hold in my hand a Hardy or Leonard reel, fondle a Vom Hofe objet d'art, go through the remains, the legacies, letters, items, belongings of old anglers who have eternally retired to the great fishing grounds in the sky. This book was a moving, enlightening, and thrilling experience for me.

To all again, my profound gratitude.

Introduction

The great fallacy shared by most fly anglers is that fly fishing is an American sport-fishing concept. Actually, fly fishing, both the concept and the practice, originated in England and Scotland, then spread to the European continent, gaining its initial foothold in France.

The earliest American fishing rods were imported from England, and the sophisticated sport of fly fishing first became nationally preeminent here in the late 1800s. Fly rods were initially fashioned from solid wood stock tapered and fabricated by hand with basic woodworking tools of the period. These early offerings were awkward, somewhat heavy, and overly long. Most of them required two-handed operation, exhibited stiff action, and were not readily conducive to fly casting.

In the 1800s a Pennsylvanian by the name of Sam Philippi innovated an all-bamboo fly rod utilizing four long strips of resilient but highly flexible bamboo laminated together into a one-piece unit. In the 1860s the concept was improved upon by Hiram Leonard, who utilized six strips of bamboo as opposed to Philippi's four.

The older or earlier fly rod versions were hand-signed, usually on the butt caps, but often on the rod shafts themselves directly above the handle or grip. Early reel seats were basic, even crude—usually a short segment at the base of the rod to which a fly reel could be affixed with cord, line, or narrow cloth or leather strips.

The reel design used in early reels has carried through to today, especially in single-action fly reel versions, though the majority of today's offerings offer better, more precise line retrieval and some of the more sophisticated hi-tech units provide automatic retrieval action.

Flies today are tied in the same manner as in the days of old, but today we have the options of miracle thread fibers as well as artificial materials that are more durable and extend the working life of the fly. Neon glow and holographic plastics also serve to make the vivid fly patterns conceivably more tantalizing to the fish species that are most often caught on fly tackle.

Since the sport is so popular and widespread and has been since its inception, there is an abundance of collectible items and materials—from fly rods and reels to fly tying materials and tools—to give the collector a well-rounded source of fly fishing collectibles. This manual will provide an overview and summation on what exists, where to find it, and, of prime importance, the values attached to collectible pieces.

FLY RODS

Fly rods are the oldest rod collectibles: They were the first rod designs originating in England, migrating with the fly fishing sport to the United States in the 1800s. Original fly rods were one-piece units of wood and were, on the average, nine feet in length. Soon, it was found that bamboo offered greater flexibility and better rod action, so rod makers began to fashion rods from four or six strips of bamboo laminated and bound together. The early bamboo rods, for the most part, also attained lengths of nine feet. It was found that a nine-foot, one-piece bamboo rod offered the most flexibility in casting and the ultimate in long cast delivery. Today, nine-footers are a rarity because they are awkward and inconvenient to travel with or store in today's compact vehicles, not because their length hampers finer casting. The lazier sports fishermen of our time prefer short or two-piece fly rods for their compactness and easy storage. Two-piece fly rods perform well but any truly knowledgeable fly fisherman will attest that one-piece rods offer better action and control of both rod and fish, and the angler who will opt for a nine-foot unit will find that he will have better casting and fly control capabilities as well as longer casting performance.

In keeping with sound tradition, today's better, more expensive fly rods are still bamboo and for the most part handmade. Bamboo was the exclusive material up to around the late forties and fifties, when it was discovered that rods

of glass or glass fiber and graphite were ideal materials for fly rods. Since the old bamboo rodsmiths
are becoming scarcer, quality rods are also becoming harder to find, so that bamboo rods of yesteryear are the cream of the fly rod collectibles.

It is widely known that bamboo provides the
best rod action of all the materials used in fly rod
fabrication. Bamboo, a tropical, canelike plant,
bends with the force of the wind to avoid breaking,
and then springs back to its upright position. Bamboo is comprised of vertical fibers growing in the
form of a tube. The vertical, steel-like fibers are
buffered from one another by a cork-type interma-
terial. As the bamboo bends, the fibers compress;
when stress is removed, the fibers and buffers
spring back with great resiliency. The ability to
spring back is a desirable quality in a fly rod.

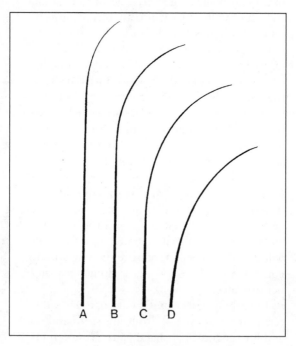

Various types of rod action...A-Fast action;
B-Medium-fast action; C-Medium action; D-Slow action

The resiliency of a particular rod and the degree of stiffness or curvature is referred to as "rod action." If the rod flexes or curves most in the upper quarter of the rod, it is said to exhibit extra quick action. If the major flexing occurs around the upper third portion of the rod, the rod is said to have fast action. Curving from the middle of the rod, the rod action can be described as medium. When a rod assumes a progressing curve all the way from the handle to the rod tip, it is termed a slow action rod.

PFLUEGER FISHING TACKLE 65
FLEW-GER

Refers to rods illustrated on page 64   *Trade Marks Reg. U. S. Pat. Office*

PFLUEGER **KING BEE** ROD

No. 2930	Length 9½ ft. Weight 6¾ oz.	Price Each $35.00

Beautiful in appearance, with action stamina and fighting qualities that make it an ideal rod for bass casting. Especially fine for handling spinners and a splendid Dry Fly Rod. Built from the very finest selection of Tonkin bamboo, heat treated, which gives it a rich Brown Tone, attractively set off by wrappings of two color silk, heavily coated with best elastic waterproof varnish.

Ferrules of nickel silver are hand welted, serrated and wound over. Reel seat aluminum and hard rubber, screw locking. Solid cork satin finish grip, shaped to fit the hand.

First guide and one tip top are Genuine Agate.—extra tip has Perfection steel top. Intermediate guides are file hard steel. Hook ring above grip.

Six strip construction—three piece with extra tip.

Packed—In a fine partitioned cloth bag and in a watertight aluminum case.

PFLUEGER **GOODYEAR** ROD

No. 2835	Length 9½ ft. Weight 6 oz.	Price Each $25.00

In appearance, action and power this rod for all around fly casting cannot be surpassed. Built with the utmost care and attention to every detail, of selected Tonkin bamboo, heat treated, which gives it a beautiful Brown Tone. Wound in two color silk, heavily coated with best elastic waterproof varnish. Nickel Silver ferrules, hand welted, serrated and wound over. Reel seat of Nickel Silver, solid cork grip satin finish, shaped to fit the hand.

First guide and one tip top are genuine agate. Extra tip has Perfection steel top. Intermediate guides of file hard steel. Hook ring above grip.

Six strip construction—three piece with extra tip.

Packed—In a fine partitioned cloth bag and in a watertight aluminum case.

No. 2836	Length 9 ft. Weight 5½ oz.	Price Each $25.00

Same as rod No. 2835 except in length and weight, a trout rod that will please the most particular angler.

PFLUEGER **SECURITY** ROD

No. 2600	Length 9 ft. Weight 5½ oz.	Price Each $15.00

For the fisherman who wants action, durability, fine appearance and long life service in a fly rod at moderate cost we recommend the Security. Made of selected Tonkin bamboo, heat treated with a rich Brown Tone, attractively wound in two colors of silk, heavily varnished.

Nickel Silver hand welted serrated ferrules, wound over. Reel seat of Nickel Silver—solid cork grip comfortably shaped.

First guide and both tip tops are genuine agate. Intermediate guides of file hard steel. Hook ring above grip.

Six strip construction—three piece with extra tip.

Packed—In partitioned cloth bag and in an aluminum case.

FOUR BROS. **DAZEE** ROD

No. 2605	Length 9 ft. Weight 5½ oz.	Price Each $8.65

A general purpose trout and fly casting rod which has power, action and fighting quality usually found only in much more expensive rods. Heat treated Tonkin bamboo, split by hand, finished in handsome brown color, attractively wound with two colors of silk, and heavily varnished.

Nickel silver roll welt ferrules. Nickel silver reel seat with solid cork cylinder grip, with hook ring above it. One tip top, also first guide, are Agatine. Extra tip has hardened steel top. Intermediate guides file hard steel.

Rod is six strip construction—three piece with extra tip.

Packed—Tips in wood form and all in a partitioned canvas bag.

A page from an old Pflueger catalog of 1934 showing rod type availability and prices of the time.

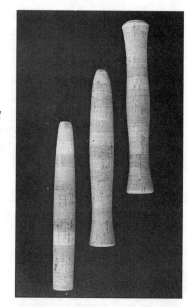

Typical fly rod handles: LEFT-*Cigar*; MIDDLE-*half Wells*; RIGHT-*full Wells*.

Handles: Fly rod handles come in a wide variety of shapes and sizes, which may be even more variable for custom-fabricated rods. The favored and best material for fly rod handles is cork. Cork is light, easily contoured by hand, and doesn't become slippery since it absorbs moisture well and dries quickly. The cork materials used as specie cork or mustard cork, specie cork being the more durable of the two.

Reel Seats: In fly rods, the reel seats are placed at the lowest point of the rod, keeping the reel well out of the way so that the fly line can be readily manipulated. Reel seats are constructed of aluminum or brass but the most resistant to saltwater or moisture corrosion is chrome-plated brass. Fly reels are easily retained on their reel seats by means of movable hoods that push or screw against the reel's feet or mounting tabs.

Ferrules: The ferrules joining two or more section of a segmented fly rod are mostly metal. Chrome-plated brass, nickel silver, and aluminum are the most common metals used in ferrule construction. The perfection of plastic fiber ferrules

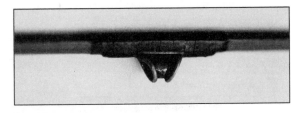

Older rods such as this Leonard sported bell-type guide.

Typical guide of the Heddon 1950s and up era.

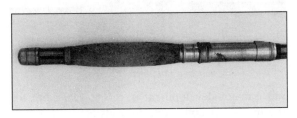

An old late 1800 Leonard rod handle.

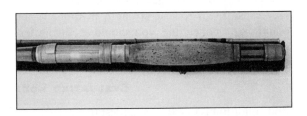

*Old Leonard rods came with sectioned cases
to hold the rod sections.*

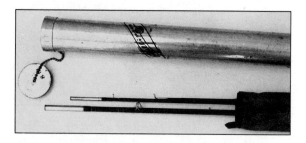

*Rods with their original cases such as this Phillipson
have a higher collectible value.*

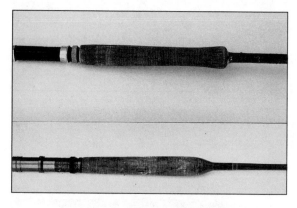

*At top is a turn-of-the-century Montague;
bottom a Phillipson "Peerless."*

was a major development in recent years, but for
the most part collectible fly rods have metal ferrules. Metal ferrules rely on friction or "hold" generated by placing the end of a male ferrule into the
accommodating end of a female ferrule. Continued
engagement and disengagement of metal ferrules
may cause them to lose strength in time. When
examining a collectible, you should see if the ferrules still retain a good, tight fit.

EVALUATING RODS

Rod condition is one of the hardest things to deter-
mine when trying to evaluate rods and their prices.
What may be excellent or mint to one collector

may be just good or possibly good to another. The age of the rod is another factor to be considered. So an old, deteriorated rod may be classed as excellent while a newer rod may not rate as high in an equally worn condition

Most of the confusion, unfortunately, is over fly rods, especially split bamboo rods. There may be defects in guides or wraps or handles and other structural parts while the bamboo blank is in A-1 condition. Most of the rods we have evaluated are listed as top grade: in good operable condition and not too roughed up.

There are many aspects to study when evaluating the condition of a bamboo or cane rod. For all intents and purposes, sectioned rods, whether two or three (rarely four), should have all the sections

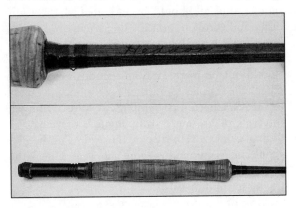

Older Heddon bamboo rods had handwritten brand names as many of the 19th and 20th century vintage bamboo offerings.

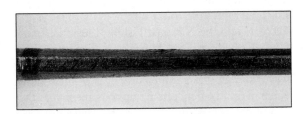

Type and signature of maker are on this collector rod. Rod was hand fabricated by H.D. Howe.

Up to the sixties one could find hand scripting on the Heddon "Pal" rods.

fairly identical in length; and the segments should be straight and true. Bends or warpage in wood rods (or cane rods) lessens their value, in some cases considerably. An untrue or crooked fly rod is a bad caster and not very controllable. All parts should be original, or only replaced by original issue fittings. Guides and guide wrappings should be original, not redone, and all should be mounted in the right order and configuration for the specific rod. Bamboo should be solidly laminated together, with no splits or spaces between laminations. Varnish should not be worn away in sections or chipped. Check the ferrules for pitting, corrosion, and cracks or breaks. Check for wrappings that are at unusual intervals or are awkwardly aligned; they may be hiding cracks or breaks in the rod. The handle should be examined for aging and wear. Check the condition of signatures, markings, logos, and identifying script or decals.

Most of the aforementioned are cosmetic checks and may not drastically detract from the appearance or functionality of the rod. The buyer must decide what his criteria for purchase are and how much he values the rod itself.

Years ago the National Fishing Lure Collectors Club devised a rod grading system, but since there are so many variables in rod condition, particularly with fly rods, the grading system is of little value. Keep in mind when looking up rods and values that conditions named in tables and lists have not been properly defined, so in many cases the collector must play it by ear.

Remember that rods with original boxes, containers, or packaging are considerably more valuable than items lacking their housing because the boxes or wraps are sometimes as rare or as valuable as the collectible items themselves. The figures presented in the rod value listing are not absolute, are subject to periodic change (usually an increase in value), and should serve as a guide to current established values.

COLLECTIBLE FLY ROD PRICE GUIDE

MAKE	DESCRIPTION	VALUE
Abercrombie & Fitch	Gene Edwards "Favorite"—8½ ft.	$275.00
Abercrombie & Fitch	H.W. Hawes—9 ft.	950.00
Abercrombie & Fitch	Payne 101—7½ ft. with tube	2,420.00
Abercrombie & Fitch	Payne 198—7½ ft. with tube	1,760.00
Abercrombie & Fitch	Payne 204—8½ ft.	1,800.00
Abercrombie & Fitch	Payne 96—6 ft.	2,800.00
Abbey & Imbrie	1920 Vintage—9 ft.	150.00
Allcock	7 ft. Bamboo	100.00
Allcock	2-Hand Salmon Rod—11 ft.	125.00
Allcock	Marvel—8 ft.	250.00
Allcock	Sapper—10 ft.	250.00
Allcock	Astoria—9 ft.	100.00
Amherst	Scarborough—8 ft.	300.00
Andrus	Presentation—8 ft.	350.00
Arnell	Gaddis—8½ ft.	50.00
L.L. Bean	Double L—9 ft.	200.00
Berkley	Bionix—8 ft.	50.00
Dame Julia Bernier	#0807—8 ft.	500.00
Lon Blauvelt	Falmouth—6½ ft.	450.00
Boyen	Cedar-Aluminum Seat—7 ft.	250.00
Brandin	4-Sided Cane—5 ft., 9 in.	1,500.00
Bristol	F-12—9 ft.	250.00
Bristol	F-7—8 ft.	275.00

Bristol	MF-18—9 ft.	250.00
Bristol/Edwards	F-18—8½ ft.	120.00
Bristol/Edwards	F-5—9 ft.	100.00
Bristol/Edwards	FB12—8½ ft.	250.00
Bristol/Edwards	FB18—9 ft.	150.00
Bristol/Edwards	FB7—9 ft.	110.00
Brookline	Sun Valley—9 ft.	100.00
J. Burdick	7½ ft.	80.00
Sam Carlson	6 Strip Bamboo—7½ ft.	2,500.00
Sam Carlson	Hex Rod—7½ ft.	3,000.00
W.E. Carpenter	7 ft.—Bag and Tube	2,500.00
W.E. Carpenter	Mahogany Proto Rare—7½ ft.	4,000.00
Clark	Custom—8½ ft.	100.00
Mike Clark	South Creek, Ltd.—8 ft.	1,000.00
Conolon	411 Fairwing—8 ft.	50.00
Constable	Fine Fly—8 ft.	150.00
Constable	Wallop Brook—6 ft., 9 in.	300.00
Constable	R.H. Woods 82—8 ft., 2 in.	300.00
Cortland	444—7 ft.	250.00
Cortland	444 LTD—8 ft.	295.00
Deerfield	Power Pak—10 ft.	120.00
Deerfield	Power Pak—7½ ft.	75.00
Dickerson	7613—7½ ft.	4,000.00
Dickerson	761510 R.B.—7½ ft.	3,800.00
Dickerson	901812-C—9 ft.	800.00
Dickerson	961913 Lt. Salmon—9½ ft.	1,300.00
Fred Divine	Black Tip, Red Wrap—9½ ft.	400.00
Fred Divine	Fairy Rod—7½ ft.	575.00
Fred Divine	Gloriwest—8 ft.	175.00
Sewell Dunton	Dark Cane—7½ ft.	175.00
Sewell Dunton	107—9 ft.	170.00
Sewell Dunton	Anglers Choice—7½ ft.	175.00
Sewell Dunton	Anglers Choice—7 ft.	175.00
Edwards	40—7 ft.	250.00
Edwards	Autograph Deluxe—8½ ft.	600.00
Edwards	Special—9 ft.	125.00
Edwards	Deluxe—8 ft.	125.00
Edwards	Deluxe—9 ft.	500.00
E.W. Edwards	Deluxe—9 ft.	500.00
E.W. Edwards & Sons	Edwards Special—8½ ft.	500.00

E.W. Edwards & Sons	Mt. Carmel—8½ ft.	350.00
Gene Edwards	Yellow Wrap, Agate Guides—7 ft.	800.00
Gene Edwards	Temwaco—9 ft.	350.00
Gene Edwards (A&F)	Favorite—8½ ft.	300.00
W.E. Edwards	34 Quadrate—8 ft.	600.00
W.E. Edwards	35 Quadrate—8½ ft.–9 ft.	450.00
W.E. Edwards	36 Quadrate—9 ft.	450.00
W.E. Edwards	40 Quadrate—7 ft.	150.00
W.E. Edwards	42 Quadrate—7½ ft.	800.00
W.E. Edwards	43 Quadrate—8 ft.	600.00
W.E. Edwards	50 Quadrate—7½ ft.	400.00
W.E. Edwards	53 Quadrate—9 ft.	500.00
W.E. Edwards	56 Quadrate—9 ft.	500.00
Farlow	369—6 ft., 3 in.	450.00
Farlow	Lee Wulff Midge—6 ft.	500.00
Farlow	Thompson Ulti—5 ft., 10 in.	300.00
Garrison	198—7 ft.	8,000.00
Garrison	212—8 ft.	2,000.00
Gillum	8 ft.—Bag & Tube	3,500.00
Bob Gorman	Green River—6 ft.	800.00
Bob Gorman	Green River—6 ft., 9 in.	600.00
Bob Gorman	Green River—7½ ft.	500.00
Goodwin Granger	Aristocrat—7 ft.	800.00
Goodwin Granger	Aristocrat—8 ft.	500.00
Goodwin Granger	Aristocrat—8½ ft.	500.00
Goodwin Granger	Aristocrat—9 ft.	400.00
Goodwin Granger	Champion—8½ ft.	400.00
Goodwin Granger	Champion—9 ft.	250.00
Goodwin Granger	Deluxe—7 ft.	1,000.00
Goodwin Granger	Deluxe—7½ ft.	900.00
Goodwin Granger	Deluxe—8 ft.	850.00
Goodwin Granger	Deluxe—9 ft.	450.00
Goodwin Granger	Deluxe—9½ ft.	425.00
Goodwin Granger	Favorite—7½ ft.	1,000.00
Goodwin Granger	Favorite—8½ ft.	500.00
Goodwin Granger	Favorite—9 ft.	450.00
Goodwin Granger	Premier—7½ ft.	1,250.00
Goodwin Granger	Premier—8 ft.	900.00
Goodwin Granger	Premier—8½ ft.	600.00
Goodwin Granger	Premier—9 ft.	500.00

Goodwin Granger	Special—7½ ft.	750.00
Goodwin Granger	Special—8½ ft.	375.00
Goodwin Granger	Special—9 ft.	400.00
Goodwin Granger	Victory—8 ft.	550.00
Goodwin Granger	Victory—9 ft.	300.00
George Halstead	9 ft.	1,800.00
Hardy	Two-Handed Salmon—10 ft.	125.00
Hardy	#5 Smuggler—7 ft.	475.00
Hardy	#7 Smuggler—9 ft., 5 in.	450.00
Hardy	C.C. DeFrance—7 ft.	400.00
Hardy	Continental Palakona—7½ ft.	350.00
Hardy	Deluxe—9 ft.	225.00
Hardy	Gold Medal—13 ft.	250.00
Hardy	Hollo Light—8 ft.	300.00
Hardy	Palakona—8 ft.	600.00
Hardy	Phantom—8½ ft.	500.00
Hardy	Marvel—7½ ft.	550.00
Hardy	Trout Fly—8 ft., 9 in.	400.00
H.W. Hawes	9 ft. Red Wrap	1,000.00
H.W. Hawes	Salmon Rod—10 ft.	450.00
H.W. Hawes	Sierra Special—9 ft.	500.00
Heddon	#10—8 ft.	300.00
Heddon	#10—8½ ft.	125.00
Heddon	#10—9 ft.	200.00
Heddon	#10 Blue Waters—9 ft.	120.00
Heddon	#10FW Blue Waters—7½ ft.	400.00
Heddon	1000 DLX Rod	300.00
Heddon	115—7½ ft.	400.00
Heddon	115—8 ft.	450.00
Heddon	115 Premier—8½ ft.	125.00
Heddon	115 Premier—9 ft.	250.00
Heddon	#125 Expert—7½ ft.	500.00
Heddon	#125 Expert—9 ft.	300.00
Heddon	#13—7 ft. Bag & Tube	800.00
Heddon	#13—8 ft.	200.00
Heddon	#13—8½ ft.	150.00
Heddon	#13—9 ft.	125.00
Heddon	#14—8 ft.	300.00
Heddon	#14—8½ ft.	175.00
Heddon	#14—9 ft.	175.00
Heddon	#14 Blue Waters—7½ ft.	600.00
Heddon	Thorobred #14—7½ ft.	750.00

Heddon	Thorobred #14—8½ ft.	175.00
Heddon	Thorobred #14—9 ft.	200.00
Heddon	#17—8 ft.	350.00
Heddon	#17—8½ ft.	300.00
Heddon	#17—9 ft.	250.00
Heddon	#17 Black Beauty—7 ft.	1,000.00
Heddon	#17 Black Beauty—7½ ft.	700.00
Heddon	#17 Black Beauty—8 ft.	500.00
Heddon	#17 Black Beauty—8½ ft.	300.00
Heddon	#17 Black Beauty—9 ft.	300.00
Heddon	#20—8½ ft.	100.00
Heddon	#20—9 ft.	150.00
Heddon	#20 Stanley Favorite—7½ ft.	700.00
Heddon	#20 Stanley Favorite—8 ft.	500.00
Heddon	#20 Stanley Favorite—9 ft.	300.00
Heddon	2030 Pal—8½ ft. (Steel)	30.00
Heddon	#35—8½ ft.	150.00
Heddon	#35—9 ft.	150.00
Heddon	#35 (1930 Model)—9½ ft.	150.00
Heddon	#35 Deluxe—8½ ft.	400.00
Heddon	#35 Deluxe—9 ft.	150.00
Heddon	#35 Deluxe Peerless—7½ ft.	900.00
Heddon	#35 Deluxe Peerless—8 ft.	500.00
Heddon	#35 Deluxe Peerless—9 ft.	300.00
Heddon	#35 Expert Tournament—9 ft.	400.00
Heddon	#36 Salmon—9½ ft.	300.00
Heddon	#40 Pal—8 ft., 8½ ft., and 9 ft. versions	20.00
Heddon	#50—9 ft.	200.00
Heddon	#50 Deluxe—9 ft.	450.00
Heddon	#50 Deluxe President—7½ ft.	1,000.00
Heddon	#50 Deluxe President—8 ft.	800.00
Heddon	#50 Deluxe President 8½ ft.	600.00
Heddon	#50 Deluxe President—9 ft.	450.00
Heddon	#51—7 ft.	1,000.00
Heddon	#55 Pal, Bass Action—7½ ft.	30.00
Heddon	#8—8 ft.	200.00
Heddon	#8—8½ ft.	195.00
Heddon	Marvin Hedge FW—7 ft.	400.00
Heddon	880 Pal—8 ft., 8½ ft., and 9 ft. versions	50.00
Heddon/Folsom	#1515—8½ ft.	150.00

Heddon/Folsom	#1515—9 ft.	200.00
Heddon/Folsom	#1520—7½ ft.	500.00
Heddon/Folsom	#1525—8 ft.	150.00
Heddon/Greenleaf	#125—8 ft.	150.00
Heddon/Weber	Deschutes Spec.—9 ft.	100.00
Herters	8 ft.	150.00
Paul Hightower	7½ ft.	300.00
Horrocks-Ibbotson	7 ft.	250.00
Horrocks-Ibbotson	Beaverkill - 8½ ft.	50.00
Horrocks-Ibbotson	Canada Creek—8 ft.	100.00
Horrocks-Ibbotson	Cascade—9 ft.	100.00
Horrocks-Ibbotson	Cascade Reg.—8½ ft.	100.00
Horrocks-Ibbotson	Governor—9 ft.	125.00
Horrocks-Ibbotson	Hudson—9 ft.	100.00
Horrocks-Ibbotson	Pack Rod—8½ ft.	150.00
Horrocks-Ibbotson	Roosevelt—9 ft.	100.00
Horrocks-Ibbotson	National Sportsman—9 ft.	100.00
Horrocks-Ibbotson	Tonka Prince—7 ft.	250.00
Horrocks-Ibbotson	Tonka Queen—7½ ft.	200.00
Horrocks-Ibbotson	Tonka Queen—7 ft., 9 in.	175.00
Gary Howells	Yellow Brown Wraps—6½ ft.	1,200.00
Gary Howells	7 ft.—Bag & Tube	1,300.00
Gary Howells	Sliding Bands—7 ft., 3 in.	1,200.00
Gary Howells	Sliding Bands—7½ ft.	1,200.00
Gary Howells	Uplocking—8 ft.	1,200.00
Gary Howells	Uplocking—8 ft., 9 in.	600.00
Gary Howells	4925—7 ft.	1,200.00
Gary Howells	Salmon Dry Fly—8 ft., 9 in.	950.00
E.M. Hunter	Approved—8½ ft.	250.00
Ingerson Tackle	Walnut Seat—6½ ft.	150.00
Ingerson Tackle	Sliding Band—6½ ft.	125.00
Ingerson Tackle	Aluminum Upblocking—7 ft.	100.00
Ingerson Tackle	Rosewood, Quad—8 ft.	180.00
Ingerson Tackle	Aluminum Seat—8½ ft.	75.00
C.W. Jenkins	Companion Rod—8 ft.	1,000.00
C.W. Jenkins	Nickel Silver—8 ft.	1,000.00
H.L. Jennings	Nickel Silver—6 ft., 2 in.	1,000.00
H.L. Jennings	Sliding Band—7½ ft.	1,000.00
H.L. Jennings	Nickel, Screw—8 ft.	950.00
Wes Jordan	Screw, Wood Seat—8 ft.	950.00
Dave Klausmeyer	Nickel Seat—7 ft.	1,000.00
Ron Kusse	Walnut Grip—7 ft.	1,300.00

Barry Kustin	American River—6 ft., 9 in.	850.00
Le Tort	Classic—7 ft.	400.00
Le Clair	Wood Seat & Grip—7 ft.	500.00
Dave Le Clair	Wood Seat—7 ft.	550.00
Leonard	Maxwell Era—7½ ft.	750.00
Leonard	1099½—8½ ft.	500.00
Leonard	2-Hand Salmon—14 ft.	400.00
Leonard	35 Catskill—7 ft.	3,450.00
Leonard	36H—6 ft.	1,500.00
Leonard	36L Baby Catskill—6 ft.	1,950.00
Leonard	37—6½ ft.	1,500.00
Leonard	37H—6½ ft.	1,300.00
Leonard	37L Baby Catskill—6½ ft.	2,500.00
Leonard	38—7 ft.	1,100.00
Leonard	38½—7½ ft.	1,750.00
Leonard	38DF—7 ft.	1,500.00
Leonard	38H—7 ft.	1,400.00
Leonard	38H Catskill—7 ft.	2,000.00
Leonard	39—7½ ft.	1,300.00
Leonard	39 Fairy Catskill—8 ft.	2,500.00
Leonard	39-4 (Hunt)—7½ ft.	2,900.00
Leonard	39H—7½ ft.	1,300.00
Leonard	39L—7½ ft.	250.00
Leonard	39M—7½ ft.	1,400.00
Leonard	40—8 ft.	1,200.00
Leonard	4099½—8½ ft.	550.00
Leonard	4099½ Salmon Dry—8½ ft.	650.00
Leonard	40H—8 ft.	1,500.00
Leonard	40L—8 ft.	1,400.00
Leonard	41H—8½ ft.	450.00
Leonard	45—9 ft.	175.00
Leonard	48—7 ft.	1,500.00
Leonard	49—7½ ft.	1,400.00
Leonard	49 Tournament—7½ ft.	800.00
Leonard	49DF—7½ ft.	1,500.00
Leonard	50—8 ft.	1,100.00
Leonard	50 Tournament—8 ft.	1,200.00
Leonard	50DF—8 ft.	1,000.00
Leonard	50DF Tournament—8 ft.	650.00
Leonard	51 (Maxwell Era)—8½ ft.	1,000.00
Leonard	51—8½ ft.	1,300.00
Leonard	51H—8½ ft.	900.00

Leonard	65—7½ ft.	800.00
Leonard	66—8 ft.	1,000.00
Leonard	700-2 Duracane—7 ft.	650.00
Leonard	850-2 Duracane—8½ ft.	550.00
Leonard	Duracane—7 ft.	750.00
Leonard	Duracane—7½ ft.	800.00
Leonard	Duracane Kit Rod—7½ ft.	525.00
Leonard	Fairy Catskill—8 ft.	500.00
Leonard	Graftek 1—8 ft.	150.00
Leonard	Graftek Special—7½ ft.	150.00
Leonard	Graftek—8½ ft.	150.00
Leonard	International Salmon—14 ft.	700.00
Leonard	LEF 60—6 ft.	100.00
Leonard	Light Salmon—9 ft.	100.00
Leonard	Parabolic—8 ft.	800.00
Leonard	Spec. Tournament Salmon—10 ft.	400.00
Leonard	Special Tournament—10 ft.	175.00
Leonard	Standard—8½ ft.	350.00
Leonard	Tournament—9 ft.	300.00
Leonard	Tournament (Hunt)—8 ft.	1,000.00
Leonard/Ausable	Downlocking	950.00
Leonard/Mills	(1920)—9 ft.	400.00
Leonard/Mills	Standard—7½ ft.	700.00
Leonard/Mills	Standard—8 ft.	700.00
Leonard/Mills	Standard—8½ ft.	500.00
Leonard/Mills	Standard—9 ft.	200.00
Leonard/Phelps	39-5—7½ ft.	1,000.00
Loomis	GT 9011—9 ft.	200.00
Loomis	IMG FR 783—6½ ft.	160.00
Richard Love	#2C—8 ft.	50.00
Lyon & Coulson	314 Crown—8½ ft.	170.00
Dave Male	Sliding Band—7½ ft.	450.00
Marshall Field	Deluxe by Heddon—6½ ft.	300.00
Maurer	Rocky Mountain Special —7 ft., 9 in.	950.00
Ron McKinley	Nickel Silver—7½ ft.	700.00
S.L. Miller	#211—8 ft.	450.00
Leonard Mills & Son	Standard—8 ft.	450.00
Leonard Mills & Son	Standard—9 ft.	350.00
Milwards	Flyfisher—8 ft.	250.00

Milwards	Salmon Rod—13 ft.	175.00
Montague	Amateur—7½ ft.	175.00
Montague	Clipper—9 ft.	100.00
Montague	Gaspe—9½ ft.	75.00
Montague	Highland—9 ft.	90.00
Montague	Rapidan—7½ ft.	175.00
Montague	Rapidan—8 ft.	150.00
Montague	Rapidan—8½ ft.	150.00
Montague	Rapidan—9½ ft.	120.00
Montague	Redwing—9 ft.	80.00
Montague	Sunbeam—7 ft.	200.00
Montague	Sunbeam—7½ ft.	200.00
Montague	Sunbeam—8 ft.	100.00
Montague	Sunbeam—8½ ft.	120.00
Cecil Musser	C 1962—8½ ft.	425.00
B.F. Nichols	Calcutta Cane—10 ft.	320.00
Orvis	Wes Jordan—8 ft.	450.00
Orvis	99—7 ft.	350.00
Orvis	99—7½ ft.	350.00
Orvis	99—8 ft.	250.00
Orvis	99—8½ ft.	300.00
Orvis	99—9 ft.	250.00
Orvis	Battenkill—6½ ft.	550.00
Orvis	Battenkill—7 ft.	400.00
Orvis	Battenkill—7½ ft.	400.00
Orvis	Battenkill—8 ft.	400.00
Orvis	Battenkill—8½ ft.	350.00
Orvis	Classic Ltd. Edition—8 ft.	800.00
Orvis	Deluxe—6½ ft.	600.00
Orvis	Deluxe—7 ft.	500.00
Orvis	Deluxe—7½ ft.	500.00
Orvis	Equinox—7½ ft.	375.00
Orvis	Equinox—8½ ft.	200.00
Orvis	Far & Fine—6 ft., 9 in.	125.00
Orvis	Far & Fine Downlock—7 ft., 9 in.	125.00
Orvis	Fullflex—8½ ft.	50.00
Orvis	Golden Eagle—8 ft., 9 in.	70.00
Orvis	Graphite—7½ ft.	130.00
Orvis	Graphite—8 ft., 9 in.	130.00
Orvis	Graphite—9½ ft.	135.00
Orvis	Impregnated—6½ ft.	600.00
Orvis	Impregnated—8½ ft.	350.00

Orvis	Light Salmon—9 ft.	300.00
Orvis	Limestone Spec.—8½ ft.	425.00
Orvis	Madison—6½ ft.	450.00
Orvis	Madison—7 ft.	450.00
Orvis	Madison—8 ft.	200.00
Orvis	Midge—7½ ft.	450.00
Orvis	Manchester—8 ft.	300.00
Orvis	Mitey Mite—5 ft.	550.00
Orvis	Pack Rod—7 ft.	750.00
Orvis	Power Flex—8½ ft.	160.00
Orvis	Rocky Mountain—6½ ft.	850.00
Orvis	Shooting Star—9 ft.	300.00
Orvis	Shooting Star Salmon—9½ ft.	275.00
Orvis	Special—8 ft.	350.00
Orvis	Special—7 ft.	150.00
Orvis	Superfine—6 ft.	750.00
Orvis	Superfine—6½ ft.	400.00
Orvis	Ultimate—10½ ft.	250.00
Orvis	Ultra Fine—7 ft., 9 in.	150.00
Orvis	Brownstone—6 ft.	700.00
Parker/Hawes	8½ ft.	1,800.00
Payne	Split Bamboo—8 ft.	2,800.00
Payne	H&F Logo—7½ ft.	2,975.00
Payne	Sliding Band—8 ft.	1,800.00
Payne	Split Bamboo—9½ ft.	700.00
Payne	104—8½ ft.	1,200.00
Payne	104 Clapp & Treat—8½ ft.	1,350.00
Payne	2-Hand Salmon—13½ ft.	400.00
Payne	2-Hand Salmon—12 ft.	550.00
Payne	200—8 ft.	1,800.00
Payne	201—8 ft.	2,000.00
Payne	202—8 ft.	2,000.00
Payne	204—8½ ft.	1,500.00
Payne	204H—8½ ft.	1,300.00
Payne	204L—8½ ft.	1,000.00
Payne	205—8½ ft.	1,400.00
Payne	208—9 ft.	1,000.00
Payne	208L—9 ft.	800.00
Payne	95-1958 B&T—6 ft.	5,060.00
Payne	98—7 ft.	3,200.00
Payne	International Salmon—12½ ft.	650.00
E.F. Payne	Blued-Split Bamboo—6 ft.	4,500.00

E.F. Payne	8 ft., 9 in.	725.00
E.F. Payne	2-Hand Salmon—15 ft.	375.00
E.F. Payne	Special—8½ ft.	1,350.00
E.F. Payne	(A&F)—9 ft.	600.00
E.F. Payne	(A&F) 405—9 ft., 3 in.	1,000.00
Jim Payne	198H—7½ ft.	2,900.00
Jim Payne	95—6 ft.	4,200.00
Payne	(A&F) 204—8½ ft.	1,800.00
Payne	(A&F) 400—9 ft.	1,000.00
Pezon et Michel	Para Royale—8 ft., 3 in.	550.00
Pezon et Michel	Parabolic—8 ft., 3 in.	400.00
Pezon et Michel	Ritz Spr Para—8 ft., 3 in.	525.00
Pezon et Michel	Salmon Red—9½ ft.	400.00
Pezon et Michel	(A&F)—9½ ft.	400.00
Pflueger	8-3380—8 ft.	25.00
Pflueger	8-6380—8 ft.	40.00
Pflueger	8-7370—7 ft.	40.00
Pflueger	8-7380—8 ft.	40.00
Pflueger	8-7386—8½ ft.	30.00
Pflueger	8-7390—9 ft.	40.00
Pflueger	8-8380—8 ft.	40.00
Pflueger	8-8386—8½ ft.	30.00
Phillipson	Fiberglass—6 ft., 4 in.	80.00
Phillipson	51 Pacemaker—8 ft.	380.00
Phillipson	Haywood Zephyr—7 ft.	400.00
Phillipson	Master—8 ft.	80.00
Phillipson	P76F—7½ ft.	150.00
Phillipson	Pacemaker—7 ft.	100.00
Phillipson	Pacemaker—8 ft.	250.00
Phillipson	Pacemaker—8½ ft.	250.00
Phillipson	Pacemaker—9 ft.	250.00
Phillipson	Pacemaker—7 ft.	550.00
Phillipson	Peerless—7½ ft.	500.00
Phillipson	Peerless Dry Fly—8½ ft.	400.00
Phillipson	Power Pakt—8 ft.	325.00
Phillipson	Power Pakt—8½ ft.	350.00
Phillipson	Power Pakt—9 ft.	180.00
Phillipson	Premium—7½ ft.	500.00
Phillipson	Premium—9 ft.	350.00
Phillipson	Smuggler—7 ft., 8 in.	750.00
E.C. Powell	B-Taper—9 ft.	450.00
E.C. Powell	Hollow Built—9 ft.	450.00

E.C. Powell	Hollow Built—9½ ft.	500.00
E.C. Powell	Steelhead—9½ ft.	800.00
E.C. Powell	Trout—7½ ft.	2,000.00
E.C. Powell	(Maslan)—8 ft.	1,000.00
Walton Powell	Alum.—8 ft.	650.00
Walton Powell	Wood Seat—8 ft.	700.00
Walton Powell	Fly—8 ft., 2 in.	600.00
Walton Powell	Fly—8 ft., 7 in.	550.00
Walton Powell	Fly—9 ft.	550.00
Walton Powell	(c. 1947)—9 ft.	300.00
Walton Powell	(c. 1950)—9 ft.	225.00
Walton Powell	Gold Signature—7½ ft.	1,100.00
Walton Powell	Legacy—7½ ft.	850.00
Rapid River	Fly—6½ ft.	125.00
E.F. Roberts	Bamboo—7 ft.	325.00
Roddy	Pro—8 ft.	20.00
Sage	496RP Graphite II— 9½ ft.	175.00
Sage	890PR Graphite II—9 ft.	175.00
Sage	Graphite II—9 ft.	150.00
Sage	Graphite III—9 ft.	150.00
Sage	Graphite IV—9 ft.	250.00
Sage	RP Graphite II—9 ft.	250.00
Sealey	Octopus—9 ft.	250.00
H.R. Sedgewick	Nickel—7½ ft.	1,000.00
H.R. Sedgewick	Blued—7½ ft.	800.00
Shakespeare	1231—7½ ft.	250.00
Shakespeare	1232—6½ ft.	300.00
Shakespeare	1233—7½ ft.	250.00
Shakespeare	1300—6½ ft.	150.00
Shakespeare	1300—9 ft.	150.00
Shakespeare	1304—8½ ft.	160.00
Shakespeare	1304—9 ft.	160.00
Shakespeare	1306—8½ ft.	160.00
Shakespeare	1306—9 ft.	160.00
Shakespeare	1307—8½ ft.	160.00
Shakespeare	1311B—8½ ft.	175.00
Shakespeare	1311T—8½ ft.	175.00
Shakespeare	1311T—9 ft.	175.00
Shakespeare	1312 Acetta—9 ft.	180.00
Shakespeare	1312B—8½ ft.	175.00
Shakespeare	1312B—9½ ft.	160.00
Shakespeare	1312T—8½ ft.	175.00

Shakespeare	1312T—9 ft.	160.00
Shakespeare	1343 Double Built—9 ft.	200.00
Shakespeare	1344 Double Built—9 ft.	200.00
Shakespeare	1344 Double Built—9½ ft.	200.00
Shakespeare	1350—9 ft.	160.00
Shakespeare	1350—9½ ft.	150.00
Shakespeare	1357—8½ ft.	100.00
Shakespeare	1360—9 ft.	100.00
Shakespeare	1360—9½ ft.	100.00
Shakespeare	1361—8½ ft.	125.00
Shakespeare	1361—9 ft.	125.00
Shakespeare	1362 (8½, 9, and 8 ft.)	125.00
Shakespeare	1363—8½ ft.	150.00
Shakespeare	1363—9 ft.	135.00
Shakespeare	1367—8½ ft.	150.00
Shakespeare	1431—9 ft.	35.00
Sharpe	Scottie—6½ ft.	300.00
Sharpe	Scottie—9½ ft.	300.00
Sharpe	Scottie Featherweight—7½ ft.	350.00
Sharpe	Aberdeen—12½ ft.	250.00
Sharpe/Farlow	Royal Tribute—8 ft., 7 in.	350.00
Vivian Shoker	Green Mountain—7 ft.	400.00
Ted Simroe	Fly—8 ft.	800.00
Ted Simroe	Fly—9 ft.	600.00
Ogden Smith	Warrior—6 ft.	250.00
W.G. Soeffker	212—8 ft.	900.00
South Bend	119 Trout Action—8½ ft.	125.00
South Bend	119 Trout Action—9 ft.	120.00
South Bend	119 Trout Action—9½ ft.	120.00
South Bend	12 (8 ft., 8½ ft., 9 ft.)	120.00
South Bend	120 (8 ft., 8½ ft., 9 ft.)	120.00
South Bend	13 (8½ ft., 9 ft., 9½ ft.)	120.00
South Bend	155 Cross Double—10 ft.	250.00
South Bend	155 Cross Double—10½ ft.	230.00
South Bend	155 Cross Double—8 ft.	260.00
South Bend	1550 Cross Single—10 ft.	220.00
South Bend	1550 Cross Single—10½ ft.	220.00
South Bend	1550 Cross Single—8 ft.	250.00
South Bend	1550 Cross Single—9 ft.	225.00
South Bend	1550 Cross Single—9½ ft.	225.00
South Bend	12 (8 ft., 8½ ft., 9 ft., 9½ ft.)	120.00
South Bend	13 (8½ ft., 9 ft., 9½ ft.)	120.00

South Bend	155 Cross Double—8 ft.	250.00
South Bend	155 Cross Double—8½ ft.	250.00
South Bend	155 Cross Double—9 ft.	200.00
South Bend	1600 Cross Single Tournament—9½ ft.	300.00
South Bend	164 Cross Double (8 ft., 8½ ft., 9 ft., 9½ ft., 10 ft., 10½ ft.)	250.00
South Bend	1640 Cross Double (8 ft., 8½ ft., 9 ft., 9½ ft., 10 ft., 10½ ft.)	250.00
South Bend	166 Cross Double (7½ ft., 8 ft., 8½ ft., 9 ft.)	300.00
South Bend	1660 Cross Single (7½ ft., 8 ft., 8½ ft., 9 ft., 9½ ft.)	300.00
South Bend	190 Cross Double (13 ft., 14 ft.,15 ft.)	275.00
South Bend	192 Cross Double (9½ ft., 10 ft., 10½ ft.)	275.00
South Bend	1920 Cross Single (9½ ft., 10 ft., 10½ ft.)	290.00
South Bend	23—8 ft., 9 ft., 9½ ft.	100.00
South Bend	24—8½ ft., 9 ft., 9½ ft.	100.00
South Bend	26—8½ ft., 9 ft., 9½ ft.	125.00
South Bend	260 Dry Fly—7½ ft.	135.00
South Bend	264 Cross Double—8½ ft.	140.00
South Bend	266 Cross Double—8½ ft.	275.00
South Bend	266 Cross Double—9 ft.	250.00
South Bend	27 Trout Action (8 ft., 8½ ft., 9 ft., 9½ ft.)	120.00
South Bend	27-8—8 ft.	325.00
South Bend	190 Cross Double (13 ft., 14 ft., 15 ft.)	250.00
South Bend	192 Cross Double (9½ ft., 10 ft., 10½ ft.)	275.00
South Bend	28 Bass—(8½ ft., 9 ft., 9½ ft.)	120.00
South Bend	29—7½ ft.	80.00
South Bend	290—7½ ft.	250.00
South Bend	291 Dry Fly—7½ ft.	250.00
South Bend	291 Pack Rod—7½ ft.	250.00
South Bend	30 Super Cross (8 ft., 8½ ft., 9 ft., 9½ ft.)	125.00
South Bend	323 Trout Action (8 ft., 8½ ft., 9 ft., 9½ ft.)	120.00
South Bend	33 Trout Action (8 ft., 8½ ft., 9 ft., 9½ ft.)	120.00
South Bend	34 Bass (8½ ft., 9 ft., 9½ ft.)	120.00

South Bend	346—8½ ft., 9 ft.	120.00
Mark Spittler	Hollowbutt Quad—9 ft.	1,000.00
Alston Spencer	1436—8 ft.	500.00
Stoddards	Trout Special—8½ ft.	200.00
R.W. Summers	275—7½ ft.	800.00
R.W. Summers	75—7 ft.	800.00
R.W. Summers	856—8 ft.	1,000.00
Thomas & Thomas	Classic—6½ ft.	800.00
Thomas & Thomas	Hendrickson—7½ ft.	1,000.00
Thomas & Thomas	Hendrickson—8 ft.	900.00
Thomas & Thomas	Light Salmon—9 ft.	800.00
Thomas & Thomas	Midge—7½ ft.	1,000.00
Thomas & Thomas	Montana—8 ft.	1,000.00
Thomas & Thomas	Bradigm—7½ ft.	1,100.00
Thomas & Thomas	Special—7 ft.	600.00
F.E. Thomas	Bangor—9 ft.	325.00
F.E. Thomas	Brownstone—7½ ft.	2,000.00
F.E. Thomas	Brownstone—8 ft.	800.00
F.E. Thomas	Brownstone (1940)	350.00
F.E. Thomas	Brownstone Special—8 ft.	600.00
F.E. Thomas	Brownstone Special—8½ ft.	400.00
F.E. Thomas	Brownstone Streamer—8½ ft.	900.00
F.E. Thomas	Dirigo—8 ft.	475.00
F.E. Thomas	Dirigo—8½ ft.	250.00
F.E. Thomas	Dirigo—9 ft.	350.00
F.E. Thomas	Dirigo—9½ ft.	300.00
F.E. Thomas	Dirigo Salmon—9½ ft.	300.00
F.E. Thomas	Dirigo Streamer—9 ft.	250.00
F.E. Thomas	Dry Fly—8½ ft.	450.00
F.E. Thomas	Fairy—7 ft.	600.00
F.E. Thomas	Mahogany Fairy—7½ ft.	4,300.00
F.E. Thomas	Special—6 ft., 8 in.	1,500.00
F.E. Thomas	Special—7½ ft.	1,200.00
F.E. Thomas	Special—8 ft.	450.00
F.E. Thomas	Special—8½ ft.	550.00
F.E. Thomas	Special—9 ft.	300.00
F.E. Thomas	Streamer—8½ ft.	700.00
F.E. Thomas	Wet Fly—9 ft.	300.00
Uslan	5 Strip Rod—7½ ft.	500.00
Uslan	9016—9 ft.	200.00
Uslan	7012 Deluxe—7 ft.	600.00
Uslan	Spencer—8 ft.	500.00

Uslan	Spencer—9 ft.	300.00
Nat Uslan	7012 Deluxe—7 ft.	600.00
Nat Uslan	Spencer, 5 Strip—8½ ft.	450.00
Vanore	Fly—7½ ft.	600.00
Vom Hofe	2-Handed Salmon—9 ft.	125.00
Edw. Vom Hofe	Uplocking—8½ ft.	400.00
Edw. Vom Hofe	Adirondack—8½ ft.	300.00
Von Lengerke	By Payne—9 ft.	650.00
Walker	Fly—7 ft.	350.00
Weber	Fly—9 ft.	150.00
Weber	1602—7½ ft.	70.00
Weber	Monogram—8 ft.	175.00
Weber/Heddon	Fly—8 ft.	350.00
Weber/Heddon	Henshall—8 ft.	450.00
Weir & Sons	Sliding Band—7½ ft.	600.00
Weir & Sons	Downlocking—8 ft.	600.00
Weir & Sons	LW/M 803—8 ft.	550.00
Winchester	Fly—9 ft.	125.00
R.I. Winston	Sliding Band—6 ft.	1,150.00
R.I. Winston	Fly—7 ft.	1,150.00
R.I. Winston	(c-1946)—9½ ft.	425.00
R.I. Winston	Hollow Built—8 ft.	850.00
R.I. Winston	IM6—9½ ft.	275.00
R.I. Winston	Leetle Fellers—7 ft.	600.00
R.I. Winston	San Francisco—8 ft., 9 in.	725.00
R.I. Winston	SW 9XXX—8½ ft.	750.00
Wright & McGill	FA Water Seal—8½ ft.	500.00
Wright & McGill	FA Water Seal—9 ft.	450.00
Wright & McGill	FB Water Seal—8½ ft.	400.00
Wright & McGill	Granger Aristocrat—8 ft.	650.00
Wright & McGill	Granger Aristocrat—7½ ft.	750.00
Wright & McGill	Granger Champion—9 ft.	250.00
Wright & McGill	Granger Champion—8½ ft.	300.00
Wright & McGill	Granger Deluxe—7 ft.	950.00
Wright & McGill	Granger Deluxe—7½ ft.	800.00
Wright & McGill	Granger Deluxe—8½ ft.	450.00
Wright & McGill	Granger Deluxe—9 ft.	375.00
Wright & McGill	Granger Favorite (7½ ft., 8 ft., 8½ ft., 9 ft., 9½ ft.)	350.00
Paul Young	15 parabolic—8 ft.	1,500.00
Paul Young	Ace—7½ ft.	450.00
Paul Young	Midge—6 ft., 3 in.	3,450.00

Paul Young	Para 15—8 ft.	2,000.00
Paul Young	Para 16—8½ ft.	2,100.00
Paul Young	Para 17—8½ ft.	1,700.00
Paul Young	Prosperity—7½ ft.	475.00
Paul Young	Special—8 ft.	600.00
Paul Young	Special—9 ft.	550.00

FLY REELS

The fly reel is the most simple of all fishing reels and is also the precursor of reels as we know them today. Before the fly reel, playing the hooked fish relied basically on keeping the fish under the rod tip and flexing and manipulating the rod itself. The flexibility of the modern fly rod still exerts the most influence on the handling of the fish, but when the flex limit of the rod is exceeded, the reel containing the line allows more line delivery in order to play the fish.

Today, because of innovations over the years, we have three types of fly reels: single action, multiplying gear action, and automatic. The original single-action reel consists of a frame, spool, and handle.

Single Action: In a single-action or simple spool reel, the diameter of the spool combined with the gear ratio determines the actual retrieval speed. The single-action reel usually features a 1:1 retrieval ratio, which means that one complete turn of line is pulled in with each revolution of the handle. To compensate for loss of retrieval speed, better single-action reels contain narrower spools or drums with wider diameters to allow quicker, higher ratio recovery.

Because of the simplicity of their design, fly reels are relatively less expensive than the more sophisticated bait casting and spinning reels. A simple drag mechanism is incorporated into the single action design to add a bit of tension

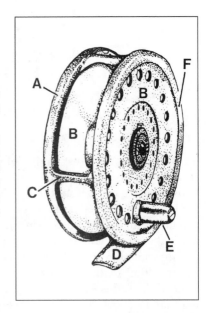

Anatomy of a single action fly reel. A-Back plate; B-Spool; C-Pillar; D-Foot; E-Handle; F-Faceplate.

to the spool action so the line will not overrun from the spool when stripping line for casting.

Another desirable, and sometimes crucial feature is interchangeable spools. This feature makes it easy to change spools to switch from a sinking fly line to a floating fly line when fishing conditions require it.

Multiplier Reels: Multiplier reels, contrary to most opinion, are not as popular with fly anglers because those marketed since their inception have not provided satisfactory or workable designs. Multipliers do, however, have good collectible value as isolated design items. For average fly fishing, multiplier reels are convenient, especially when low weight is desired to minimize casting fatigue. The best multiplier reel designs have a 2:1 retrieval ratio.

Automatic Fly Reels: Automatic reels allow mechanical line retrieval with prewound mechanisms that, when spring-loaded and activated by a finger release, retrieve the line quickly. They come in vertical mount and horizontal mount, one's preference being governed by personal taste. The drawback to automatic reels is their excessive weight, which tends to inhibit control and balance when fly casting. Automatic reels also have a limited line capacity, which is not desirable when long casts are needed. Line sizes no bigger than number 6 are strictly recommended.

Fly reels mount on the bottom-most part of the rod below the grip so that they do not interfere with casting. Their primary function is to play the fish and assist in its landing. Basic fly reels are reversible mount; they can be mounted with the handle on the right or left. A right-handed caster will prefer to have the handle on the left so that he does not have to change hands as a fish is hooked. A left-handed person will prefer the opposite.

Fly Line

In all forms of casting, save for fly casting, it is the weight of the lure, bait, or sinker that propels the line. Artificial flies are virtually weightless, so it is the fly line that delivers the fly which is achieved by propelling or working the line back and forth to produce enough velocity to shoot it through the air. Air friction tends to rapidly absorb the power generated by casting the line. To get the most out of the energy generated, the line must be designed so that maximum velocity is maintained for the longest time.

There are three forms of lines: level taper, weight forward, and double taper. The double taper is easiest to handle, and when one side wears because of use, it can be reversed in the reel. Fly lines vary in weight and should be selected according to the action of the rod: slow, medium, or fast action.

Old fly lines, from the earliest types to those of the late fifties, are great collectibles, and if found mint in original packaging do have some value, though less than values of more sophisticated fly fishing collectibles. Special sinking lines, particularly the original sinking lines made in England in

1938, are rarer and are valued as collectibles. The originals were of silk braided over bronze wire. However, since they failed to perform well, their popularity waned and they were not manufactured in great quantity.

In the late fifties a feasible sinking line was developed with the introduction of Dacron. The sinking lines from those years are collectible. Though some fly lines are collectible, they are the least popular of fly fishing collectibles.

REELS IN RETROSPECT . . .

Fly reels first took their place in fishing history in 1770 when Onesimus Ustonson created the first specimen, a brass multiplier, which was included in a kit of later manufacture that was presented to King George IV around 1828 in London, England. His basic design was the forerunner of single-action fly reels as we know them to this day. Ustonson was a well-known tackle maker of his day, and when he died in 1810, the business passed to his son, Charles. After Charles's early demise in 1816, the business was left to his wife, Maria, who saw that the business went on as usual under the Ustonson name until the mid 1800s.

In the annals of fly reel history the elder Ustonson first made mention of the multiplier reels and the reel stop mechanism, though he does not take credit for their inception. So we must assume that he was carrying on, modifying, and improving an existing design theory. In the last quarter of the eighteenth century reels for fishing, offshoots of Ustonson's design, came into general and widespread use.

The early reel design soon found its way to America, and the Colonial period saw the birth of a new and eager breed of fly fishers, starting off with fly reels imported from the mother country as early as 1773, three years before the colonies gained their independence from England.

It has been widely accepted by historians that

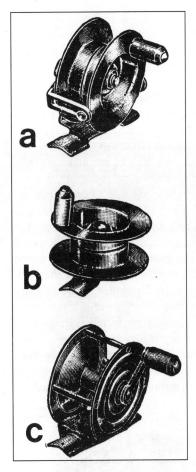

Early unknown fly reels with small spools typical of early prototypes. Cuts from Shapleigh catalog.
(Courtesy: Carl F. Luckey)

reels reached an early peak in popularity during the latter part of the eighteenth century. The origins of the tackle and tackle makers of this era are sketchy, resulting in no clearcut criteria for identifying early reels of this period. There are, however, a number of distinctive features that can be used to identify the early, more primitive reel offerings.

For one thing, iron was used almost exclusively in reel structure themselves or to reinforce some early renderings in wood. Many early reels had one short foot that was used for tying to or screwing into existing rods. Few, if any, early reel versions were signed or identified as to maker and locale.

Early reel manufacturers, or reelsmiths as they were known, were primarily jewelers or clock and watchmakers who had the machinery to turn out precision reels. Talented reelsmiths started off by producing reels for themselves and soon found them in demand by friends and discerning anglers. Initial reel offerings were rarely signed and this factor alone gives them a certain mystique, a mystique quite palatable to serious collectors.

Though the halcyon days of reelmaking are of great interest and fascination to collectors, it is the nineteenth century that spawned a host of innovative collectible angling pieces that most intrigue tackle collectors. The great technological developments and production methods of the nineteenth century spurred the growth of the fishing tackle industry. Of course we must also consider that fishing was becoming a most popular outdoor sport, rivaled only by hunting.

In 1808, T. Williamson perfected a design for a 9x multiplying reel. Williamson's new design placed the reel handle in the center of the reel, making it more confined in the circumference of the reel and at the same time making the handle

Early 1800s reel; origin and maker unknown.

Unknown "Peanut" single action.

less prone to damage. Williamson's original design also exhibited the first click mechanism, though Williamson did not incorporate the click mechanism in his own reels. Early multiplier reels did have some technical and operational shortcomings, and in 1841 the single action again became widely preferred.

In the early 1800s the Birmingham reel was conceived, considered to be the prototype of the select fly rod as we know it today. One of the early Birmingham reels was manufactured by James Haywood, a brass worker, listed in Birmingham in 1815 as a producer of reels, ferrules, and other brass bric-a-brac. After his death, his widow, Mary, carried on operations together with her son, James. The Haywood reels were actually not true Birmingham style reels, but old-fashioned, larger spooled multipliers and stop-locking single-action types that the new Birmingham style reels were rendering obsolete.

Because of new manufacturing facilities made possible by the Industrial Revolution, the new British Birmingham reels were manufactured more cheaply and in greater quantities. The initial Birmingham reels were constructed of brass without a click and sported curved handles with an ivory or

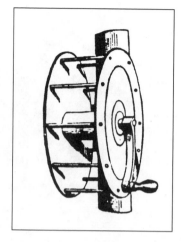

*Birmingham style
reel considered
the true ancestor
of the fly reed.*
(Courtesy: American
Museum of Fly Fishing)

bone handle and a conventional reel foot or mount.
They featured narrow spools and, while essential to
both fly and bait fishing, gained wider acceptance
for fly fishing. This early style of fly reel was produced in quantity throughout the nineteenth century, making identification and dating of unsigned
or unmarked samples quite difficult.

In the mid 1800s, another innovative refinement
was added to the Birmingham reel: a raised checkplate. The checkplate was an external integrated
disc-type housing on the backplate of the housing
of the click mechanism. The accessing checkplate
allowed the fisherman to repair, replace, adjust, or
oil the working mechanism of the reel without dis-
assembling the whole reel. The raised checkplate
was a weighty additive and soon fell out of favor in
the 1870s but was modified, improved upon, and
reintroduced in the United States by lawyer-fisher-
man-historian Henry P. Wells. The new Wells reel
of lightweight aluminum captured the fancy of
Julius Vom Hofe, who produced the version from
1889 to 1911.

Responding to complaints that the Birmingham
reel's handle tended to interfere with and foul up
line, yet a new design was incorporated in which
the handle was directly attached to the side plate of
the drum. This modification was instituted as early

as 1867. In this period also, the development of the revolving plate took place. In the revolving plate reel, the handle attached to the revolving plate, doing away with the miniature windlass used for retrieval.

Another new material found its way into reel structure, ebonite, known in manufacturing circles as black hard rubber. Easy to work and shape, ebonite was lighter than metal and particularly useful in the makeup of larger reels where weight reduction was essential. Reinforced with brass or nickel silver, these revolving plate reels are coveted by collectible buyers for their quality, craftsmanship, and overall aesthetic beauty.

Another style of reel that prevailed during the mid 1800s was the Nottingham reel. This primarily wooden reel was a light, free-running spool type made of either walnut or mahogany. The Nottingham reels, named after the city of Nottingham (also

At the top is a Nottingham reel; bottom a classic Leonard raised pillar unit of German Silver.

Nottingham reel broken down to show the then primitive but effective gear drive.

made famous in the Robin Hood epic), were not fly fishing reels but mainly designed for river fishing. They were, however, drafted into fly fishing use by a wide number of fly fishermen. In time, the early, cruder wood models were improved upon by adding metal back reinforcement, brass handle bearings, adjustable checks, and line guards. While these reels were manufactured well into the 1940s, they have an antique quality that makes them favored collectible items.

A metal rim and a backplate were Nottingham additions; a metal rim was placed on the inside of the backplate, and a metal piece served as the inner plate of the spool. These innovative variations were introduced by David Slater and incorporated into the Nottingham design, which was thereafter known as Slater's Combination reel. Slater received an English patent on his new design on May 22, 1883. The new patented design included a reel that combined the metal pillars of the conventional reel with the exposed front rim of the Nottingham design.

The aerial reel conceived by Henry Coxon, also of Nottingham, England, was an 1895 invention that was quickly sold to Samuel Allcock, who patented the design under his name on March 26, 1896. The aerial design is historically attributed to Allcock, though it was copied and elaborated on by other reel makers of the period.

*Two exceedingly rare Conroy reels from one of the older arti-
san reelmakers. Both reels together are valued at $10,000.*

The aerial reel is lightweight, 3½ inches to 4½
inches in circumference, and narrow spooled with a
distinctively spoked drum somewhat emulating a
bicycle wheel. The aerials were a shade on the frag-
ile side but well suited to fly fishing. They were fabricated from combined materials, which mostly
included wood, aluminum, hard rubber, and Bake-
lite, and were in production for over fifty years.
The finer aerials are also designated as Match reels
since they were frequently used in contests or
matches. Match reels are similar in shape and
styling to standard fly reels of the narrow-spool
variety, but Match and aerial reels rotate freer as
the spool revolves only on the tip of the center pin
thus generating less friction or drag.

Peter Malloch innovated and perfected his own
reel style, the Sun and Planet reel, in the mid 1850s.
Malloch's design prevented the plate or arm from
being turned around on the axis of the reel at the
time the line is being run out. The handle could also
be used to retard line runout if and when required.

Abercrombie and Fitch considered Malloch's
reel a fly reel. However used, the reel was an excel-
lently crafted and attractive item fabricated from
German Silver-bound bronze with a black hard
rubber backplate. In 2¼- to 5-inch reel diameters,
the Sun and Planet reel was featured and sold by
Abercrombie and Fitch for $12 to $15.

Old reels such as this circa 1906 reel have greater collectible value if found with original case.

Hardy is eminently and widely known for fly reel excellence. Early Hardy Perfect reels fetch as much as $5,000 on the auction market. The Perfect is most likely the first fly reel to incorporate ball bearings and the first to feature a distinctive agate line guide. The fabulous Hardy reel line was first presented by the tackle company in the 1880s. The Hardy brothers are best known for the "Perfect" model but at least twenty-five other models and designs were manufactured and marketed. Hardy reels rate high as fly collectible items. The older models especially fetch top dollar on the auction and collectible market. Our collectible reel table

At the right is the Hardy Lightweight; left-Pflueger Medalist 1498.

Meek #50 from a historic reel-maker.

will list the various Hardy reel models and their respective price values.

On May 12, 1874, Charles F. Orvis patented his trout reel, with its narrow spool and perforated sideplates. The double handle made it popular with anglers for quicker retrieval.

The Meeks of Frankfort, Kentucky, were mainly interested in producing the Kentucky Reels, bait casting mainstays, but were also instrumental in producing some of the finest fly reels of the mid 1800 era. Another reel maker not known for the manufacture of single-action fly reels, J.R. Sage of Lexington, Kentucky, is believed to have produced click reels for bass fly fishing.

William Billinghurst was a famed gunsmith of his day, but in 1859 he took out a patent for his famous reel, which collectors refer to as the Bird-cage reel. The Billinghurst reel was the fourth fishing reel to receive a patent. The Birdcage reel was able to recover line as quickly as a multiplying reel and a lot quicker than standard single-action fly reels.

The Orvis 1874 patent reel is recognized as one of the most popular and the standard of American fly reels, enjoying popularity and sales for a period of about forty years after its inception. As the Billinghurst reel is sometimes considered the grandfather of American fly reels, the Orvis can

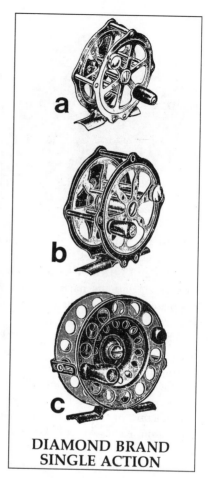

Three old Diamond reels... A is a brass unit, skeleton frame with removal spool, 4 oz. in weight. B is a lightweight fly reel of nickel silver. C is another brass unit finished in black lacquer, wood handle, and metal ball balance weight. Cuts are from an old Shapleigh catalog.

**DIAMOND BRAND
SINGLE ACTION**

take the credit for being their father. Early models were of nickel silver, featured a hollow spindle, had no click mechanism, and the bottom of the foot was hand-engraved: C.F. Orvis maker, Manchester, Vermont, pat. May 12, 1874. The spindle was profusely perforated for air penetration which aided in allowing built up line moisture to escape. The reel was of riveted construction and underwent ongoing development resulting in a number of distinct models, including a wider version for bass fly fishing. It is widely held that all the 1874 Orvis patent reels were manufactured by the Man-

Offerings from a 1928 Pflueger catalog.
TOP: *Pflueger "Golden West." Nickel silver and hard rubber construction.*
MIDDLE: *Pflueger "Hawkeye" with adjustable tension.*
BOTTOM: *Pflueger "Progress" with one piece perforated backplate. Featured easy disassembly.*
(Courtesy: Shakespeare)

hattan Brass and Manufacturing Company of New York City.

The raised pillar design reel was another fly reel innovation, and though most historians credit Hiram Leonard with the original design concept, it was substantiated that James Ross was responsible for an earlier version of the raised pillar design. The raised pillar reel may have originated in England but the design was not as popular overseas as it was in the United States.

The first raised pillar reel to achieve success was the Leonard version originally patented by Francis

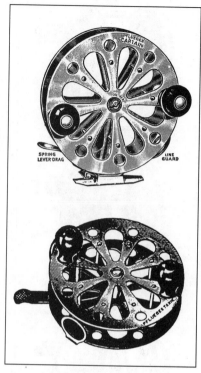

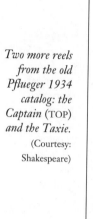

Two more reels from the old Pflueger 1934 catalog: the Captain (TOP) and the Taxie.
(Courtesy: Shakespeare)

J. Philbrook, with rights assigned to Hiram Leonard when the patent was issued. By 1900 Leonard-type reels were being produced in quantity in the New York City shop of Julius Vom Hofe, who continued to build the Leonard reels up to the second world war.

The Leonard style reel has long been a choice piece favored by both anglers and collectors. It is aesthetically appealing and the impact of the Leonard name has made this type of reel highly prized by collectors.

Mass production and the specialization and labor allowed early mass producers of reels and tackle like Hendryx Vom Hofe, Chubb, Meisselbach, and Pflueger to flourish. These people came upon the scene all at once, offering unlimited quantities of inexpensive to medium-priced reels for a widening fishing market.

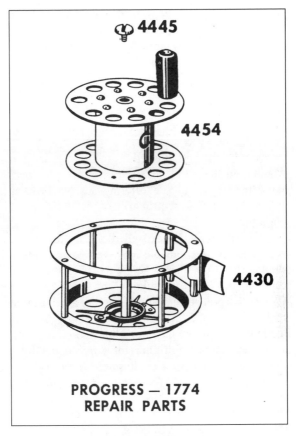

Breakdown of the Pflueger 1774 Medalist.

Some of the finest reels turned out during the Industrial Revolution were by the Vom Hofe family. In the late 1800s Edward Vom Hofe turned out quality reels of impeccable design, on a limited basis, from a shop in New York City that employed three workers. The beauty and excellence of the Vom Hofe reels make them the classics of their age, and most think that the Vom Hofe reels are to American angling what the Hardy reels are to British angling.

The patriarch of the Vom Hofe family, Frederick Vom Hofe, had five children, two of whom,

Julius and Edward, became the mainstays of the reel and tackle business. Frederick began the business in 1857 and was joined in 1860 by his first son, Frederick, his second son, Julius, and his third son, William. The early reels, rare collectibles, were stamped "F. Vom Hofe and Sons, maker." By the time of Frederick's retirement in 1882, Julius had built his father's reel making shop into a highly profitable business.

Soon Edward established his own tackle shop in Manhattan, near Fulton Street, featuring his own saltwater reels and the offerings of his brother Julius. The reels were primarily of nickel silver and ebonite.

Edward Vom Hofe expanded into producing fly reels and was responsible for seven basic models: the Peerless (No. 355), a freshwater click reel; Cascapedia (No. 413) for salmon and steelhead; the Griswold (No. 496), a multiplier and adjustable reel; the Tobique (No. 504) with a central revolving handle shaft; the Colonel Thompson (No. 484), an offset handle multiplier for salmon; the Restigouche (No. 423), an adjustable drag reel for salmon; the Perfection (No. 360) for trout and bass.

A brass and hard rubber reel by Julius Vom Hofe.

Three rare collectibles. TOP TO BOTTOM: *Vom Hofe #100; Allcock Redichen; unknown early English.*

Left—Rogan Ballyshannon; right—Pflueger (circa 1900).

*Meisselbach
"Rainbow"
#631.*

LEFT: *unknown German Silver;*
RIGHT: *Heddon 125 "Imperial."*

*Young
"Pridex"
0234.*

LEFT: *John Emery 107*; RIGHT: *Hardy St. John (England).*

Montgomery Ward 150 Sport King.

Different fly reels have varying line capacity, the larger the circumference, the bigger the line size or length capabilities.

AUTOMATIC FLY REELS

Maligned by many, the auto fly reel has been greatly criticized and is selected by very few for serious fly fishing. For one thing, they are excessively heavy and difficult to precision cast with. Secondly, many of them are side mount types that mount awkwardly in the fly reel seat. Many purists wonder why they were conceived or used at all. Their only virtue is fingertip-fast line retrieval.

The first automatic fly reel patent was given to Francis A. Loomis on December 7, 1880. In 1881 half the rights were assigned to a James Plumb, and the Syracuse, New York, firm of Loomis, Plumb and Company was established. Sometime in the mid 1880s the company was sold to Yawman and Erbe, who continued to issue automatic fly reel models based on the Loomis design. In 1888 Phillip Yawman further improved the design, making the reels smaller, lighter, more durable, and

Martin Automatic (Spapleigh catalog).

Meisselbach Automatic (Shapleigh catalog).

Pflueger Automatic.

Early Shakespeare Automatic.

Perrine Automatic.

more effective in operation. Yawman and Erbe were absorbed by the Horrocks-Ibbotson Company of New York, and though the new owners continued automatic reel production, they fell victim to very strong competition by the Martin Automatic Fishing Reel Company of Mohawk, New York, which today remains one of the largest manufacturers of automatic fly reels.

The classic Fin-Nor "Wedding Cake."

Fin-Nor 1960 collectible #3.

The following listing encompasses virtually all the known fly reels that have become collectible items; some rare, others more commonly available. Prices may fluctuate, but the values listed are very close to market value and for the most part "right on the money."

FLY REEL VALUES

Brand	Type; Model	Value
Abbey & Imbrie	25 yd	$ 65.00
Abbey & Imbrie	Hardy look-alike	100.00
Abel	#5, 3" Black	290.00
Abel	#5, Adjustable Drag Nylon case	295.00
Abel	#0, 2¾" Black	240.00
Abel	#1, 3¼" Black	325.00
Abel	#5 Bluewater	1,000.00
Abel	TR-1 Black	250.00
Abel	TR-2 Gold Frame	335.00
Abel	TR-3 Black	275.00
Abercrombie & Fitch	Hardy Featherweight	120.00
Abercrombie & Fitch	Hardy Flyweight	145.00
Abercrombie & Fitch	Yellowstone	25.00
L. Ackerman	#8234	50.00
Allock	Aerial	125.00
Allcock	Aerial 3½"	425.00
Allcock	Marvel 3¾"	50.00
Allcock	Marvel 4"	95.00
Allcock	Conquest	745.00
S. Allcock & Co.	Gilmour 3⅛"	85.00
S. Allcock & Co.	3" by J.W. Young	95.00
Ambassadeur (Sweden)	3" Trout	80.00
R. Anderson & Sons	Brass Salmon 4¼"	130.00
Angler	Rainbow-Greg Spool	15.00
A.P.I.	Black 2x Spool	495.00
A.P.I.	Black 3¾" Anti-Reverse	525.00
A.P.I.	Special Limited Ed. (only 100 made)	400.00
A.P.I.	Spring Creek with pouch	260.00
Appleton & Bassett	Fly, 2¼"	165.00

Arnold Bivens	Green, Wide Spool	20.00
Arnold Products	Allison, 4″ Adj. Drag	195.00
Ath	F3, Lake Taupo	275.00
Ath	Rio Orbigo, 3½″	325.00
L.L. Bean	#10	30.00
L.L. Bean	#77	25.00
Berkley	#510	15.00
Pat Billinghurst	Model I, 1859 3½″	1,600.00
Pat Billinghurst	Birdcage 1859	11,500.00
Pat Billinghurst	Model II—3″	700.00
Pat Billinghurst	Brass Birdcage	1,540.00
Wm. Billinghurst	1859 Patent	795.00
Bivans	Green, 3¾″, 3 pos. Drag	25.00
Blackhawk	Auto Fly	15.00
Bogdan	Black 3¼″ Goldcase	1,100.00
Bogdan	0 Salmon Multiplier	1,700.00
Bogdan	00 Multiplier 3½″	1,650.00
Bogdan	300m Salmon, 3¾″	1,850.00
Bogdan	Baby Trout	1,550.00
Bogdan	Steelhead, 3⅜″	1,295.00
Bogdan	300 Salmon Multiplier	1,150.00
Bogdan	Trout, 3¼″ "S" Handle	1,550.00
Bogdan	Steelhead 3¼″	1,500.00
Bogdan	Wide Trout, 3¼″	1,450.00
S.E. Bogdan	Black Narrow Trout 3¼″	1,500.00
S.E. Bogdan	Small Narrow Trout, 2¾″ Gold	1,500.00
Brass	1¾″ with Stop Latch	275.00
Brass	Ball Handle, 2⅛″ Rare	220.00
Brass	Ballhandle 3″	150.00
Brass	Small, Machined Brass	120.00
Brass	40-yd., Counterbalanced	60.00
Brass	Tiny 25-yd. Collar Fitted	120.00
Brass	Primitive, Ball Handle	220.00
Brass	Skeleton Fly / Black Enamel	10.00
Duncan Briggs	#2	12.00
Bristol-Horton	#65 Anodized 3½″	30.00
Bristol-Horton	#65 Black Enamel 3½″	25.00
Bronson	#360 Royal	25.00
Bronson	#380 Multi-Royal	30.00
Bronson	#390 Royal Matic	20.00
Bronson	#560 Royal, 3⅜″	25.00

J.A. Burkholder	#PKT Trout	75.00
Herb Butler	Standard Fly	30.00
Carlton	Ideal	65.00
Carlton Mfg. Co.	Fly—Standard	45.00
Conroy	#5 (tiny) Silver	250.00
J.C. Conroy, N.Y.	Nickel Silver	495.00
Thomas J. Conroy	#3, Nickel Silver	375.00
Thomas J. Conroy	JVH Pat. 1989	495.00
Cortland	3¼″	12.00
Cortland	Pro Crest 3½″	35.00
Cozzone	60-yd. 2¼″	225.00
Cozzone	Midge Fly	245.00
Cozzone	80-yd.	275.00
L.M. Dickson	Maginot	30.00
Briggs Duncan	Fixed Check, 3⅜″	40.00
Briggs Duncan	Black, Constant Check	15.00
Briggs Duncan	#2	12.00
Edwards	#30, 2⅞″	15.00
Edwards	#40, 3¾″	10.00
Edwards	#40, Aluminum	20.00
Farlow	Brass Guard, 2⅝″	280.00
Farlow	Cobra 3½″	100.00
Farlow	Python, Adj. Drag	100.00
Farlow	Python, 4″ Salmon	100.00
Farlow	Sapphire 3⅛″	50.00
Harrison Felton	Archangel, 4¼″	1,200.00
Harrison Felton	LittleWing II, 3⅝″ (Only 5 manufactured)	1,100.00
Fenwick	Class 4, 3¼″ Gold, Black	350.00
Fenwick	Class 4, Gold, Aluminum, Black	450.00
Fenwick	Class 6, Trout 3½″	150.00
Feurer Bros.	Gold Seal, 3¾″	175.00
Fin-Nor	#1, 3″ Bag & Box	350.00
Fin-Nor	#1, Trout Reel with Pouch	350.00
Fin-Nor	#1, Tycoon	900.00
Fin-Nor	#2, Early Wedding Cake	700.00
Fin-Nor	#3, Anti-Reverse 3¾″	295.00
Fin-Nor	#3, Wedding Cake 4″	850.00
Fin-Nor	#1, 3″ Post Wedding Cake	320.00
Fin-Nor	#2, 3⅛″ Post Wedding Cake	320.00
Fin-Nor	#3 Second Model 3⅝″	325.00

Fin-Nor	#3 Wedding Cake	725.00
Fin-Nor	Wedding Cake, 4″ Garwood	1,150.00
Finlay-Falkirk	Trout Reel, 3¼″ Aluminum	170.00
Ashbourne Foster	All Brass Birmingham Type	80.00
Four Brothers	Delight 40-yd.	155.00
Four Brothers	Delight 60-yd.	120.00
Gayle	#2, Simplicity	25.00
Gayle	#6, Simplicity	25.00
Hardy	Birmingham, 2⅜″ Brass	450.00
Hardy	Bougle, 3¼″	1,750.00
Hardy	Altex #1 Mark V	150.00
Hardy	Altex #2 Mark III	130.00
Hardy	Altex #3 Mark V	150.00
Hardy	Birmingham 2⅜″ Brass	450.00
Hardy	Bougle, 3¼″	1,750.00
Hardy	Cascapedia 7 Position Drag	5,900.00
Hardy	Cascapedia, Black Anodized	3,900.00
Hardy	Featherweight, 2¾″	160.00
Hardy	Flyweight, 2½″	100.00
Hardy	Gem 3¼″	180.00
Hardy	Golden Prince 4¼″	300.00
Hardy	Hercules (early), 2½″	1,000.00
Hardy	Hercules Trout, Brass, 2½″	1,000.00
Hardy	Husky, 3¼″	125.00
Hardy	Husky Salmon, 3⅜″	200.00
Hardy	Husky Salmon, Silent Drag	170.00
Hardy	Lightweight, 3⅛″	100.00
Hardy	Longstone, 4½″	200.00
Hardy	LRH	120.00
Hardy	LRH Early Model	250.00
Hardy	LRH Lightweight, 3³⁄₁₆″	200.00
Hardy	Marquis #10, 3⅞″	120.00
Hardy	Marquis #5, 3″	125.00
Hardy	Marquis #6, 3¼″	125.00
Hardy	Marquis #7	100.00
Hardy	Marquis #8, 3⅝″	100.00
Hardy	Marquis Salmon #1, 3⅞″	120.00
Hardy	Marquis Salmon #2, 4⅛″	125.00
Hardy	Perfect, 2¾″ Wide Drum (1905)	750.00
Hardy	Perfect, Brass Face, 2⅝″	1,200.00
Hardy	Perfect, Black, 2⅞″	180.00
Hardy	Perfect, Agate, 2⅞″	600.00

Hardy	Perfect, 3⅛″, Extra Spool, Agate	150.00
Hardy	Perfect, Narrow Drum (1905)	850.00
Hardy	Perfect, Brass Face Drum, 3¾″	1,500.00
Hardy	Perfect, Enamel Finish, 3⅝″	145.00
Hardy	Perfect, Maroon	230.00
Hardy	Perfect, Narrow Drum (1922), 3⅜″	395.00
Hardy	Perfect, rare Red Agate, 3⅜″	1,100.00
Hardy	Perfect, White Ceramic Line Guide, 3⅝″	185.00
Hardy	Perfect, Red Ceramic Line Guide, 3⅜″	175.00
Hardy	Perfect, Ebonite Knob, 3⅝″	280.00
Hardy	Perfect, Salmon, Wide Spool, 3½″	495.00
Hardy	Prince, 3″	170.00
Hardy	Princess, 3½″	125.00
Hardy	Scientific Angler, 4″ Extra Spool	150.00
Hardy	Scientific Angler, Marquis Copy, 3″	175.00
Hardy	Scientific Angler, Adj. Drag, 3″	150.00
Hardy	Silex #2, 4″	250.00
Hardy	Silex Major	350.00
Hardy	Sovereign, Gold; Adj. Drag, 2¾″	275.00
Hardy	Special Perfect, 3¼″	500.00
Hardy	St. Aiden, 3¾″	200.00
Hardy	St. Aiden Salmon, 3¾″	150.00
Hardy	St. Andrews, 4⅛″	200.00
Hardy	St. George, 2 9/16″, Aluminum	550.00
Hardy	St. George, Enamel Finish, 3″	300.00
Hardy	St. George, White Agate, 3″	600.00
Hardy	St. George, Jr., Enamel, 2 9/16″	400.00
Hardy	St. George, Jr., White Agate, 2 9/16″	700.00
Hardy	St. John, 3⅞″	165.00
Hardy	St. John, Brass Ribbed Foot, 3⅞″	120.00
Hardy	St. John, Aluminum Foot	125.00
Hardy	St. John Salmon, Late	100.00
Hardy	Sunbeam, 2¾″	150.00
Hardy	Sunbeam, Wire Line Guide, 3″	250.00
Hardy	Super Silex, 3¾″	450.00
Hardy	Davy, Brass Foot, 3½″	2,500.00
Hardy	Elarex, Level Wind	250.00
Hardy	Hydra, Single Pawl	50.00
Hardy	Uniqua, 2⅝″	200.00
Hardy	Uniqua, 2⅞″	120.00

Hardy	Uniqua, 3⅛″	125.00
Hardy	Uniqua, 3⅜″	140.00
Hardy	Uniqua, 3⅝″	125.00
Hardy	Uniqua, Von Lengerke & Detmold, 3½″	110.00
Hardy	Uniqua, "OK" 9, 3⅛″	125.00
Hardy	Uniqua Salmon, 3¾″	300.00
Hardy	Viscount #130	100.00
Hardy	Viscount #150	100.00
Hardy	Zenith, 3¼″	195.00
Hardy	Zenith, 3⅜″	170.00
Harris Reel	Gloversville, N.Y.	350.00
Hart	Marquesa (1970)	200.00
Hart	Limpqua Marquesa	250.00
Hart	Limpqua Salmon	300.00
Hart Reel Co.	Marquesa, Black & Chrome (1978), 3¾″	625.00
Haskell	2¾″	500.00
Haskell	Narrow Spool, 3⅜″	450.00
Heddon	#125 Imperial, 3¼″	150.00
Heddon	#340, 3¾″	35.00
Heddon	#37, Auto Fly	25.00
Heddon	#5, Auto Fly	80.00
Heddon	#57, Auto Fly, Bronze	30.00
Horrocks-Ibbotson	#1106	20.00
Horrocks-Ibbotson	#1107 Rainbow	25.00
Horrocks-Ibbotson	Utica Auto Fly	10.00
Horrocks-Ibbotson	Vernley Trout	35.00
Horton-Meek	#54, 2¹⁵⁄₁₆″	135.00
Horton-Meek	#55, 3⅛″	150.00
Horton-Meek	#56, 3⅜″	125.00
Ideal	#2	75.00
Langley	Riffle, 3¼″	35.00
Lawson	#1 Laurentian	15.00
Lawson Machine Works	#2 Laurentian, Black	20.00
Leonard	Light Salmon, 3⅝″	600.00
Leonard	Fairy Trout	1,100.00
Leonard-Mills	"Mills" Name 2¾″	695.00
Leonard-Mills	#48, 3¾″	495.00
Leonard-Mills	#50, 3⅛″	900.00

Leonard-Mills	#50 Trout, 3″	700.00
Leonard-Mills	Midge, 2⅜″	1,200.00
Leonard-Mills	Midge Click	750.00
Leonard-Mills	Salmon, 4¼″	600.00
Leonard-Mills	Trout Reel by Julius Vom Hofe	950.00
H.L. Leonard	Bi-Metal, Brass, 2⅜″	1,400.00
H.L. Leonard	#191813 Patent, 2⅝″	900.00
H.L. Leonard	Salmon, 4¼″	500.00
H.L. Leonard	Click Reel-Trout, 2⅛″	1,700.00
Leonard Mills & Son	Aluminum Spool, 3¾″	500.00
Martin	Auto Fly (1923) Silver	25.00
Martin	Auto Fly (Black)	15.00
Martin	#72 Boxed	50.00
Martin	#63, 3″	25.00
Martin	#77W, 3¼″	35.00
Martin	Miracle Matic #500 Auto	20.00
Martin	Special Presentation Auto	400.00
Meek	#55, Black, 3⅛″	70.00
Meek	#56, 3¼″	100.00
Meisselbach	#17 Partly Plated	20.00
Meisselbach	#17 Expert, 1896 Patent	50.00
Meisselbach	#19 Expert, 2½″	70.00
Meisselbach	#19 Expert, Nickel Plated Brass	75.00
Meisselbach	#19 Expert (1886) Mini Fly Reel	60.00
Meisselbach	#250 Featherlite	50.00
Meisselbach	#260 Featherlite (1904 Patent)	50.00
Meisselbach	#260 Featherlite, Blue Brass	40.00
Meisselbach	#280 Featherlite	50.00
Meisselbach	#290 Featherlite, 1904 Patent, 3″	60.00
Meisselbach	#370 Airex	65.00
Meisselbach	#372 Simploreel	50.00
Meisselbach	Automatic	35.00
Meisselbach	Aluminum Auto, 1914 Patent	60.00
Meisselbach	Amateur, 2¼″	50.00
Wm. Mills	Dry Fly Salmon, 3⅛″	600.00
Wm. Mills	Fairy Trout, Vom Hofe	300.00
Wm. Mills & Son	Julius Vom Hofe 1896 Patent, 2¼″	100.00
Wm. Mills & Son	Kennett Reel 1920, 3″	250.00
Millward	Flymaster, 3½″	50.00
Millward	Flycraft, 3½″	80.00

Montgomery Ward	Sport King, Black, 3″	25.00
Montgomery Ward	#60-6414 Hawthorne, 3¼″	40.00
North Fork	Trout Fly, 2⅞″	170.00
Ocean City	#36, Black, 3½″	20.00
Ocean City	#36, Black Enamel, 3⅜″	15.00
Ocean City	#90 Automatic	20.00
Ocean City	Viscoy, 3″	20.00
Ocean City	Brass & Aluminum, 3″	120.00
Orvis	1874 Model, 2⅞″	600.00
Orvis	Batten Kill, 2¾″	70.00
Orvis	Batten Kill, with Case	90.00
Orvis	Batten Kill, 3¼″	60.00
Orvis	Batten Kill, Mark III, 3½″	85.00
Orvis	Batten Kill, Mark IV	100.00
Orvis	Batten Kill, Mark V, 3½″	100.00
Orvis	CFO 123, 2⅞″	120.00
Orvis	CFO II	100.00
Orvis	CFO III, 3″	120.00
Orvis	CFO IV, 3¼″	90.00
Orvis	CFO Trout, 3″	165.00
Orvis	CFO Trout, 2″	195.00
Orvis	Commemorative 1874, 2⅞″	380.00
Orvis	DXR, 3⅛″	175.00
Orvis	Green Mountain II, 3⅜″	75.00
Orvis	Presentation EXR II, 3″	75.00
Orvis	Presentation EXR III	125.00
Orvis	Presentation EXR, IV, 3½″	165.00
Orvis	Presentation EXR V, 3¾″	150.00
Orvis	SSS 11/12, 4″ Multiplyer	335.00
Billy Pate	Salmon, Black, Suede Case	275.00
Peerless	#1, 2¾″	320.00
Peerless	#1½, 3″	350.00
Peerless	#2 Trout, 3¼″	350.00
Peerless	#2A, 3¼″	450.00
Peerless	#3, 3¼″	450.00
Peerless	#3A, 3¼″	430.00
Peerless	#5, 3¼″	450.00
Peerless	#5 Salmon	450.00
Peerless	#6, 3½″	600.00
Perrine	#30 Free Stripping	25.00
Perrine	#50 Automatic	15.00
Perrine	#50 Free Stripping	25.00

Pflueger	#1492 Medalist, 2⅞″	45.00
Pflueger	#1492 Medalist Double Pawl (1930)	100.00
Pflueger	#1494 Medalist (early)	75.00
Pflueger	#1495 Medalist, 3½″	40.00
Pflueger	#1496½ Medalist (early)	100.00
Pflueger	#1496 Medalist	30.00
Pflueger	#1498 Medalist	35.00
Pflueger	#1554 Trout	35.00
Pflueger	#1554 Salmon, Trout	20.00
Pflueger	#1558 Salmon, Trout, 5½″	35.00-50.00
Pflueger	#1558 Large Trolling Fly	25.00
Pflueger	#1592 First Model; Rare	175.00
Pflueger	#1595 RC Medalist	30.00
Pflueger	#1774 Progress, 2⅞″	25.00
Pflueger	#264 Hawkeye, 2½″	225.00
Pflueger	Golden West, 60-yd.	200.00
Pflueger	Golden West, 80-yd.	225.00
Pflueger	Hawkeye, 60-yd., 2½″	200.00
Pflueger	Hawkeye, 80-yd.	175.00
Pflueger	Progress, 60-yd.	65.00
Pflueger	Progress Bulldog, 80-yd.	50.00
Portage	Seminole, 2¾″	50.00
Portage	Seminole, 60-yd.	60.00
Precisionbilt	Mosquito, 3″	50.00
Precisionbilt	Silver Moth	75.00
Carlton Rochester	Automatic, 1889 (1903 Pat.)	40.00
Rome	2 in 1 Automatic (1907 Pat.)	130.00
Ross	#30310 Trout, 3⅜″	85.00
Ross	#3.5, 3⁷⁄₁₆″	125.00
Ross	Cimmaron C-3, 3½″	100.00
Ross	Gunnison G-2, 3¼″	220.00
Ross Reels	Heritage, 2⅞″	1,400.00
Ross, Etna, Ca.	#53 Black, 3⅝″	140.00
Scientific Angler	#1112 System 3	600.00
Scientific Angler	Model 12/13	185.00
Scientific Angler	Sys. 11 by Hardy, 4″	150.00
Scientific Angler	Sys. 5 by Hardy, 3″	150.00
Scientific Angler	Model 45L	90.00
Scientific Angler	Sys. 4	90.00
Scientific Angler	Sys. 4 by Hardy	125.00

Scientific Angler	Sys. 6 by Hardy, 3¼″	50.00
Scientific Angler	Sys. 8, 3⅝″	70.00
Scientific Angler	Sys. 8 by Hardy	120.00
Scientific Angler	Sys. I, 3½″	45.00
Scientific Angler	Sys. II, 3½″	135.00
Scientific Angler	Sys. II, 3¾″	125.00
Shakespeare	#1821 Auto	10.00
Shakespeare	#1821 OK Auto	10.00
Shakespeare	#1821 Model D Auto (horizontal)	10.00
Shakespeare	#1822 Wondereel Auto	25.00
Shakespeare	#1824 Free Strip Auto	25.00
Shakespeare	#1835 Tru Art Auto	25.00
Shakespeare	#1837 Automatic	20.00
Shakespeare	#1837 Silent	25.00
Shakespeare	#1864 Au-Sable	25.00
Shakespeare	#1864 Russell Fixed Click, 3″	25.00
Shakespeare	#1895 Russell, 3½″	15.00
Shakespeare	#1896 Russell	40.00
Shakespeare	#1900 Steelhead (1936)	85.00
Shakespeare	#2531, 3⅝″	30.00
Shakespeare	#7594 Purist, 3¼″	25.00
Shakespeare	Alpha	25.00
Ogden Smith	Aluminum-Brass, 3″	125.00
Ogden Smith	Brass, Gun Metal, 4½″	350.00
Ogden Smith	Flyos, 3″	70.00
South Bend	#1100 Reno	15.00
South Bend	#1100B Oreno	20.00
South Bend	#1105	20.00
South Bend	#1110	20.00
South Bend	#1115	20.00
South Bend	#1120 Orenomatic Auto	20.00
South Bend	#1122 Finalist	20.00
South Bend	#1125 Orenomatic Auto	20.00
South Bend	#1126 Orenomatic Auto	20.00
South Bend	#1130D Orenomatic Auto	25.00
South Bend	#1140 Orenomatic Auto	20.00
South Bend	#1150 Orenomatic Auto	20.00
South Bend	#1165 Oreno, 3½″	25.00
South Bend	#1165 Oreno, Maroon, 3½″	35.00
South Bend	#1170 St. Joe	25.00
South Bend	#1175 Oreno	20.00

South Bend	#1180 St. Joe	20.00
South Bend	#1185	25.00
South Bend	#1190	30.00
South Bend	#1195	25.00
South Bend	(Like Hardy Perfect) 3⅝″	70.00
Sport King	#57, 3″	15.00
Sport King	#64 Auto	20.00
Sterling		25.00
Tagren	Re-Treev-It	25.00
Terry	1871 Patent, 1⅞″	125.00
Thomas & Thomas	Classic	230.00
Union Hardware	#7169, 3″	25.00
Union Hardware	Sunnybrook, Brass	15.00
Valentine	89, Disc. Drag	80.00
Edward Vom Hofe	#355 Peerless	2,200.00
Edward Vom Hofe	#355 Peerless Trout	2,000.00
Edward Vom Hofe	#355 Peerless #3, 2⅝″	1,400.00
Edward Vom Hofe	#360 Perfection, 2¾″	6,500.00
Edward Vom Hofe	#423, 4″	1,000.00
Edward Vom Hofe	#423 Salmon	800.00
Edward Vom Hofe	#423 (1883 Pat.)	700.00
Edward Vom Hofe	#423 Custom, 3¾″	1,200.00
Edward Vom Hofe	#504 Tobique	900.00
Julius Vom Hofe	Raised Pillars	600.00
Julius Vom Hofe	Aluminum, 3⅜″	500.00
Julius Vom Hofe	Crown, 3″	350.00
Julius Vom Hofe	Fairy Fly, 2¼″	600.00
Von Lengerke & Antoine	Size 3 Fly	175.00
Von Lengerke & Detmold	Hardy Uniqua style, 2⅞″	140.00
Walker	#200 Salmon	1,100.00
Walker	#300 Multiplier	1,000.00
Walker	TR-1	1,300.00
Walker	TR-2	1,000.00
Walker	TR-3, 3⅛″	900.00
Walker	TR-3 Trout, 3⅛″	1,000.00
A.L. Walker	#200 Salmon	1,300.00
A.L. Walker	#300 Salmon	975.00
Arthur Walker	#100, 3¾″	900.00
Arthur Walker	#100 Salmon, 3¾″	1,200.00
Wards	#60-6414 Hawthorne, 3¼″	25.00

Wards	#61 Auto	15.00
Wards	Precision Auto	15.00
Weber	#566, Silent Knight	25.00
Weber	Kalahatch, 3⅜″	30.00
Weber	Trout Reel, 3½″	15.00
Wells	3″ Fly	100.00
Winchester	#1136 Raised Pillars	100.00
Winchester	#1135 40-yd.	120.00
Winchester	#1235 60-yd.	90.00
Winchester	#1421 80-yd.	50.00
Winchester	#1418, Brass	100.00
Yawman & Erbe	Auto (1880 Pat.)	100.00
Yawman & Erbe	Auto (1891 Pat.), 3″	60.00
Yawman & Erbe	Auto (1891), 2¼″	60.00
J.W. Young	Salmon, Black, 3½″	90.00
J.W. Young	#1505, 3½″	80.00
J.W. Young	#1520, Grey	50.00
J.W. Young	#1530, 3½″	100.00
J.W. Young	Beaudex Small, 3″	70.00
J.W. Young	Beaudex, Grey, 3½″	60.00
J.W. Young	Beaudex, 3¾″	70.00
J.W. Young	Beaudex, Wireline Guide	60.00
J.W. Young	Beaudex, 4″	60.00
J.W. Young	Condex, 3¼″	55.00
J.W. Young	Condex, 3⁷⁄₁₆″	70.00
J.W. Young	Pridex, 3½″	60.00
J.W. Young	Pridex, 3¾″	60.00
J.W. Young	Rapidex, 4″	125.00
J.W. Young	Rapier Graphite, 3¼″	25.00
J.W. Young	Rapier Narrow, 3¾″	25.00
J.W. Young	Voldex, 3″	150.00
J.W. Young & Sons	Ambidex #2	50.00
J.W. Young & Sons	Beaudex	75.00
J.W. Young & Sons	Pridex	100.00
J.W. Young & Sons	Rapidex	140.00
J.W. Young & Sons	Seldex	60.00
Otto Zwarg	#300 Screwhandle, 3½″	1,200.00
Otto Zwarg	#300 Aluminum Fort, 3½″	900.00
Otto Zwarg	#300 7 Position Drag, 3⅝″	1,000.00
Otto Zwarg	#400 Tiny Multiplier	1,700.00
Otto Zwarg	#400 Multiplier, 3¾″	1,000.00
Otto Zwarg	#400 Laurentian	1,500.00

| Otto Zwarg | #400 Salmon, 3¾″ | 1,000.00 |
| Otto Zwarg | Multiplier Salmon, 3½″ | 1,500.00 |

Listed above are the major manufacturers and reel suppliers of products that have become collectible items. A few minor offerings may have been overlooked, but for the most part this is a most comprehensive list. Values may vary according to what the seller is asking and what the buyer is willing to pay. Besides, prices of collectibles fluctuate, usually going up in value. Whenever possible, we have listed sizes of the reels after name, description, or model number to give you a more accurate idea as to the circumference of the reel.

FLIES

Flies unfortunately must be categorized as lesser collectibles. Though there are many flies, old flies, thousands of them, they can very rarely be identified by the maker or manufacturer or origin. Exceptions are collection pieces or sets documented as produced by the legion of quality flytiers and artisans. Of course some designs and patterns are strictly innovations and creations of select professional flytiers but again, unless documented, one has no way of knowing if the fly is a creator original or a copy by a veritable flytier.

No phase of lure making is as unique or esoteric as fly tying, a rewarding craft and a great hobby for anglers and lure buffs. With all the thousands of types conceived and marketed, the basic standard designs have remained and flourished through the years. Basically, there are two forms of flies: dry flies and wet flies, with all other deviations (larvae, nymphs, pupae, spiders, beetles) falling into one or the other category. Dry flies are fished above water and are designed to float. Wet flies on the other hand are designed to be fished under the surface of the water. The objective of both types is to imitate by color or shape the form of insect a particular trout, bass, or salmon readily feeds on. Streamers are another form of fly bait and their function is to imitate various fledgling fish forms.

Fly tying tools and materials on the other hand have excellent collectible value, especially the earlier, more simplified fly tying vises,

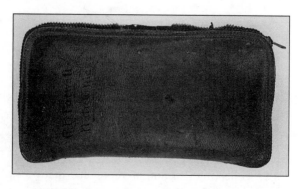

Old Fly pouch with owner's name about fifty years old.

Older fly pouches were three-tiered and lined with sheepskin to anchor hook ends. This one is a zippered leather version.

A rare double hook salmon fly, origin unknown.

Top is a rare L.L. Bean salmon fly, mint condition in original package. Bottom is a similar fly of unknown origin. The packaged piece has higher collectible value.

Three more rarities: top and middle by L.L. Bean; bottom by S. Allcock, another great name in fly tackle history.

Rare packaged fly by Milwards. In their day they went for twenty cents. Today some collectible flies will fetch hundreds.

hackle pliers, scissors, bobbins, etc. Many of these are also considered antique collectibles.

Fly collectibles are a rare segment simply because some of them are virtually unidentifiable. Perusing the pages of Langs catalog will unearth some choice fly items.

In their recent edition a select Carrie G. Stevens "Upper Dam Me" (F.R.S.) fancy pattern fly on a #6 hook with original card and cellophane, unused, was up for $200. One of the most famous flytiers was Frederick Halford. Some dry flies from the Harold Mott collection, with letters of authenticity, in excellent condition are being auctioned for $500 to $600. A Mike Poche May Fly Nymph with authenticity card is fetching up to $150. A set of Sam Slaymaker II Little Brook, Little Brown, and Little Rainbow streamer flies with dated letterhead is going for $300 to $400. All these and other rare offerings that surface from time to time can be obtained from Langs.

FLIES AS COLLECTIBLES

Mention of the first commercially available hooks came in John Denny's *The Secrets of Angling*, first published in 1613. The earliest commercial hooks were produced in "Merry Old England," and the first maker credited was Charles Kirby. He invented the particular hook bend that bears his name to this day.

The eye hook made of the newly innovated versions were made by Allcock's of Reddick in 1867, and was popularized by Henry Sinclair Hull in 1877. The only major hook modification was Cholmondeley Pennell's down-eyed hook.

The hook serves as the foundation of the fly and all the naturally imitating entities that go into the physical makeup of the wet fly, streamer, nymph, midge, etc., are built up around the shank of the hook from the eye back to the rear of the hook shank just before the shank begins its "hook" curve.

As I mentioned, it is extremely difficult to evaluate and verify specialty collectible flies without paper identification, as flies cannot be signed. Some characteristic oddities may clue the collector to the origin or creator of the fly, but here again one may be chasing phantoms.

Coveted collectible flies are designs by their tying originators and, if authenticated, are the ones considered collector's gold. The following are some of the great innovators and tiers whose flies you should be on the lookout for.

To fly fishermen and fly collectors, Harry and Elsie Darber are considered elder statesmen and venerable flytiers. In 1928, Harry Darber started a career as a professional flytier. He married Elsie after she worked for him as an assistant, and they both produced standard style flies and their own innovations in great quality, their flies being much in demand by serious fly fishermen. One of the flies they are known for is the Horrible Matuka, a low-water salmon fly tied on a #2 hook. These original Darbees are becoming scarce and valuable.

Bonnie and Rene Harrops are responsible for such classic flies as the Double-Wing Sidewinder, and Bonnie's Poly-Wing Spinner. Bonnie specializes in tying wet flies, spinners, and nymphs, while Rene confines his artistry to duns, no hackle, and standard western dry fly patterns. Their list of customers has included famous American anglers and corporate accounts such as Orvis.

Dave Whitlock specializes in damselflies and dragonflies, and his specialty is the Damsel Wiggle nymph into which he has successfully incorporated materials that help produce the necessary natural wiggling action induced by damselflies to propel themselves in the water. Whitlock's wiggle nymphs are tied on 7957B or 3906 in sizes 8, 10, 12, and 14. His workmanship is precise, lifelike, and highly valued. The Hair Gerbubble Bug is another of his creations.

Darwin R. Atkin is responsible for the Mari-Boo series of Steelhead flies imparting a good drifting action controlled by both water current and the fisherman's rod action. Atkin's famed Mari-Boo series included the Streaker, Pole Kat, Daisy, Bright Ember, Dark Ember, Chaquita, Bloody, and Sunburst. The Mari-Boos are tied on nickeled or gold hooks in sizes 2–8.

Raleigh Boaze, Jr., evolved newer dimensions in fly fabrication, being one of the first to utilize latex and similar rubberlike substances to create body imitations of pupae, grubs, and larvae specialty flies including stone and mayfly nymphs. His original Caddis is a fine fly and a welcome addition to any collection as well are all his earlier offerings.

The great Vincent Marinaro took a scientific approach to fly tying and his innovative killer designs are some of the best flies ever created. His study of the life and habits of terrestrial insects enabled him to recreate fly specimens that were not only unique but highly effective. Marinaro is credited with originating such patterns as the Green Drake Dun, Green Drake Spinner, Hendrickson Dun, Hendrickson Spinner, Sulphur Dun, Sulphur

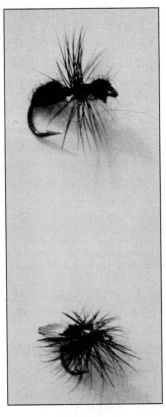

Two rare collectible originals by Vince Marinaro: the Black Ant (top) and the Aphid.

Spinner, Light Olive Dun, Dark Olive Dun, Black Ant, Dark Red Ant, Double Jassid, Jassid, and Pontoon Hopper. Marinaro also wrote the book, *A Modern Dry Fly Code*, which is a collectible item along with his very rare and valued flies.

Helen Shaw was the matriarch, first lady, and queen of flytiers. This consummate fly tying artist tied all types of flies, all of which have become high-level and rare collectibles. Her superb book, *Fly Tying*, also a collectible, was one of the standard textbooks for fly tying beginners. For the most part her fly tying was restricted to collectors only and there are very few but rare framed specimens of her limited edition flies and streamers.

Art Flick, master flytier, also took a scientific approach to fly tying. The fly had to be constructed

*A Doug Swisher original. Swisher was one of the
earlier tiers to utilize rubber legs as outriggers in some
of his dry fly creations.*

in such a way that it wouldn't flap on its side after
hitting the water surface, wouldn't tail dip or bit
eye first. Flick specialized in dry flies, though he
could and did tie other fly fishing versions. He
could master and tie any standard fly and his workmanship was superb. Flick also wrote some enlightening books on the subject of fly angling; namely:
*Art Flick's Streamline Guide to Naturals and their
Imitations* and *Art Flick's Master Fly Tying Guide.*
Some of his classic dry flies include: the Hendrickson, the Red Quill, and the Grey Fox Variant.

Doug Swisher and Carl Richards were a potent
fly fishing team, and they were instrumental in cre-
ating some revolutionary fly patterns when older
dry flies weren't giving them the success they
sought. Both parties continually experiment with
new patterns, both are excellent tiers, and both
have patterns that are known and accepted
throughout the world by fly fishing aficionados.
Their famous patterns include: the Grey Olive No-
Hackle, the White Black Hen Spinner, the No-
Hackle Dun.

Ernest Schweibert, superb fly fisherman and
well-known author, is an expert flytier as well and
has created many spectacular salmon flies. His
quality tied flies include such classics as the Dusty
Miller, the Half-Stone, the Lady Caroline, the Sil-

Lee Wulff, another fly tier, and some of his highly crafted flies. Top is the standard Royal Coachman; middle, his Grey Wulff; bottom, his Brown Wulff.

ver Grey, the March Brown, the Atherton Squir-reltail, the Orange Blossom, the Hairwing High-lander, the Pale Torresh, the Minktail, and the Hairwing Onset. His widely read books include: *Matching the Hatch, Salmon of the World, Remembrances of Rivers Past.*

Ted Niemeyer is an astute fly fisherman, one of the greats, and has consistently used and applied every imaginable fly representing the nymph stage of common terrestrial flies. Niemeyer's nymphs and wet flies are classics, and he has originated a few of his own patterns. He is known for his meticulousness and the delicate quality of his flies. Some of his famous flies include his Niemeyer Caddis, Catskill coiler (dark), Badger, and Peacock and Atherton mediums. Niemeyer flies are choice and sought after collectibles.

BASS BUGS AND POPPERS

This category contains poppers or popping bugs which are small cork-bodied feathered lures used with a fly rod for capturing bass and similar species. The standard bug rod is larger than the average fly rod since the poppers, being larger than standard flies, are somewhat more air resistant. Bug tackle must be proficient enough to overcome the air resistance of a stocky lure. There are many types of bass bugs available; some custom made, some manufactured by leading tackle suppliers in quantity. A

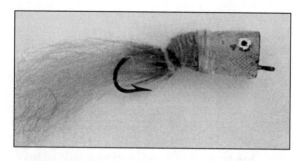

An old Bass Popper, turn of the century, origin unknown.

well-designed, effective popper will have a concave or dished face allowing the bug to dip or shoe under the surface and make a popping sound or bubble that serves to entice bass or panfish. Bullet-head bugs differing slightly in design from poppers are just as effective with their collar feathers, buck-tail bodies, and long streamer feathers. Poppers and bugs are effective fly lures, particularly in shallow water and offshore situations.

Since poppers and bugs have been standard products for many tackle manufacturers, there are a good many that are common issues and are readily identifiable. These models can serve as bona fide collectibles, the older ones naturally garnishing greater values.

Early bass bugs were handcrafted by the same individuals who tied flies. The feathers and hackles were the same used for flies, but the bodies were shaved and shaped from cork, many folks utilizing old bottle corks. Cork was the ideal body material as it is virtually weightless and floats readily. Usually the fly feather work and hackles were first tied to the hook. Then the shaped cork body was slit lengthwise and placed along two-thirds of the length of the hook. The corks were flat-bodied or concave up front, flat or at an angle, tapering to the hackle and feather sections. The bodies were glued on the hook. They were always painted bright colors, spotted, and decorated to entice fish to strike.

Some of them were painted natural colors to simulate frogs and similar pond life. Old bugs, like old flies, were subject to destruction from the teeth and jaws of fish, so if they were fished, they were usually damaged and valueless.

Unless you find manufactured bugs by older firms that are boxed, packaged, bagged, and unused, it is almost impossible to identify and categorize them. Really old lures of this type are virtually unidentifiable unless accompanied by authenticating papers or documents.

$\mathcal{O}$LD CREELS

To a great many fly fishermen, creels were essential for holding freshly caught fish. They were usually of wicker, woven loosely so they could be submerged in water, thus keeping fish alive for extended periods while other fish were caught and added to the stock in the creek. The following is a list of collectible creels that are much sought after and coveted by fly collectible buffs.

A.E. Nelson	14″ Split Willow, 5″ × 8″ Zipper Pocket	$1,200.00
A.E. Nelson	15″ Split Willow, Red, Coarse Weave	850.00
A.E. Nelson	Orange, Snap Handle	550.00
Clark	14″ Split Willow	750.00
Clark	15″ Split Willow	1,200.00
Frisbie	16″ Green Wicker	2,500.00
George Lawrence	16″ Green Split Willow	450.00
George Lawrence	15″ Green Split Willow	650.00
George Lawrence	14″ Orange, Leather Trim	450.00
George Lawrence	Large Size—Tooled Leather Handle	600.00
Haywood Fish Keeper	Leather Hinged Split Wicker	550.00
Joseph Schnell	16″ Split Willow, Red	1,800.00
Macmonies	Zipper Top, 16″ Wicker Basket	2,000.00
Turtle	Sliding Latch—Rattan	1,800.00
Turtle	Leather Bound Ilhan	7,500.00
Turtle	Whole Willow, Turtle Latch	550.00
Turtle	14″ Whole Willow, Raffia Lid Rim	1,500.00

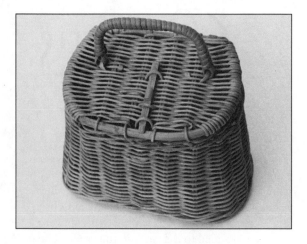

A rare and old worm creel.

Worm creels were specifically used to contain worms and keep them fresh and alive in moistened earth.

*Standard mid to late 1800s creel, origin unknown,
value around $1,000.*

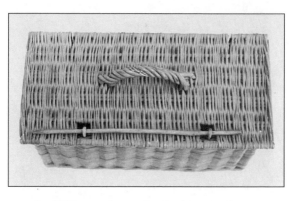

An old Victorian box creel, value $1,500 to $2,000.

The old Victorians were spacious and strong; today very rare.

Another old creel dating back many decades.

FLY FISHING COLLECTIBLES —WHERE TO FIND THEM

Those of you who chose to buy this concise but informative mini-manual have decided to purchase it for a number of valid reasons, some of which pertain to your specific interest. You may want it for the necessary documentation of value listings; you may want it to introduce yourself to the specifics of fly fishing collectibles; or you may wish to find out how to buy or add to a collection. This section will serve as an aid to locating and obtaining choice and available collectibles.

Estate sales, particularly those of large families that go back a century or more, can offer a wealth of hand-me-down collectible items. Or maybe the estate owner happened to be a fishing collectible enthusiast who amassed a large inventory of select or carefully chosen valuables. Many fly fishing collectibles, particularly fly rods, also have high values in the field of antiques. Special estate brokers are well versed on the values of fly fishing collectibles, so the items will sometimes be rare and always high in price. If money is no object to the fly fishing collector, estate sales will provide the buyer with some desirable items of high quality, usually in very good to good condition.

If you frequent antique shops, continued visits should at some time or other yield a wide spectrum of angling collectibles. Antique dealers are well versed in the current values of antiques, or have access to such values in research sources and books that list coveted and high-ticket items. Even when a visit to an antique shop may be fruitful, keep in mind that this is one source where the prices will be on the high side, with the seller not very willing to bargain or haggle on a fixed price.

If you are vacationing or travel a lot, check out hardware and collectible shops in old, small out-of-the-way towns. Towns in New England or around the central southern states can become sources of exceptional old and valued prices. Older hardware or tackle shops handed down from generation to generation may have shelves or back rooms with hoards of goodies, some even unused and in their original boxes or packaging. If the proprietors are not cognizant of their values, you may be able to pick up items at low to moderate prices. If the owner is shrewd, sharp, and up with the times, you may have to part with more scratch than you anticipated.

Garage sales may occasionally offer some items that are of value, but most of these sales only yield current, well-used gear as opposed to artifacts. However, the prices are usually real bargains as the homeowners are only trying to liquidate items to eliminate clutter or ones that they do not wish to pack and move. Now and then you can get lucky at a garage sale.

Flea markets and swap-shops offer a plethora of collectible fly fishing items from mint to well used. They are ideal and successful places for searching out fly rods, fly reels, flies, and assorted fly fishing accessories. Swap-shop vendors frequently accumulate their inventory from individual sellers, pawnshops, shop inventory sellouts, and thrift shops. The major objective of the swap-shop or flea market vendor is locating low-ticket wares to resell for whatever they can get. Another pertinent factor: The vendor is rarely cognizant of fly fishing collectible values; angling gear is just more stuff to peddle. To the knowledgeable buyer who has researched the going price of particular collectible items, this type of sales outlet can yield untold treasure at low, low prices.

Private collectors are another source, and they will periodically place sales notices in local and regional newspapers and in national fishing and sportsmen's magazines. The collectibles or collections they list will fetch the highest market values but the quality of their offerings are unique as well as first rate. You will pay top dollar but keep in mind that collectibles do increase in value and sooner or later you will realize a return on your investment; values predestined to escalate.

Occasionally, pawnshops will get fishing tackle that may have some collectible value. Fly rods and reels generate some reasonable pawn dollars, although far below market values as pawnshop proprietors are reluctant to part with their money and are aware of the pawner's need. Even with their pawnbroker's markups, angling items can be discovered in pawnshops at reasonable prices.

At this point I am going to pass on to the reader a most valuable source unknown to most collectors: Tom Greene. Greene is the owner of Custom Rod and Gun in Lighthouse Point, Florida. An astute and highly knowledgeable collector, Tom Greene has amassed the greatest and biggest collection of fishing collectibles in the world. I know for I have seen it with my own eyes. Greene not only has every fly fishing collectible imaginable but he has them in ample quantities. Fly rods of the masters, fly reels from Meek, Meisselbach, Hardy . . . you name the make and model and Greene will have it. Since Greene's collection is so ample and diversified he is a qualified collectible dealer and his duplicate items are for sale to serious collectors. Dropping him a line at Custom Rod and Gun or giving him a call at 1-800-940-4886 may enable you to acquire that special rare piece you are looking for but haven't found to date.

AUCTIONS

Auctions are a primary source of fly fishing collectibles, and there are special auctions held all over the country specifically for collectible items.

Langs Sporting Collectibles, Inc., is the country's leading tackle auctioneer and their home base is Boxborough, Massachusetts. For annual auction locations you can contact Langs at (508) 635-1840. The company deals in all forms of fly fishing collectibles and gets large quantities of it for auction. Rods, reels, lures, creels, knives, tins, tackle boxes, and a host of related gadgets.

A buyer's premium of 13% is applied to the winning bids of all property sold, to be paid by the buyer. A 13% discount will be offered for cash or check payments resulting in a 10% buyer premium. This serves as a commission based on the auction price, paid to Langs by the seller. A number of the main auctions are held at locales in the Boxborough, Massachusetts area.

Prior to each auction, Langs puts out a massive auction catalog listing newly acquired and older inventory. The price of each catalog is $25. People are encouraged to prebid on any items in the catalog by mail or phone. If the prospective buyer is not outbid, he will become the new owner of the article bid upon. Pieces are listed by number and the Lang catalog is profusely illustrated.

Through this outlet one can have access to specialty collectible fly rods by Leonard, Mills, Paul Young, Thomas and Thomas, Winston, Payne, Orvis, Hardy, Heddon, South Bend, and Tycoon. A host of collectible fly rods is available from $50 to over $2,000.

Langs also keeps a running stock of choice collectible fly reels. Reels by quality manufacturers and craftsmen such as Otto Zwarg, Edward Vom Hofe, Julius Vom Hofe, S.E. Bogden, Fin-Nor, Ross, Hardy, Mills, Meisselbach, Meek, Abbie and Imbrie, Winchester, Shipley, and Bogden are also represented and made available.

Old creels also show up now and then in their inventory, and you can have access to old style Turtle creels and Indian style wicker creels, and every so often some rare early Victorian creels will surface (which have values up to $3,000).

If you are buying, selling, consigning, or requesting appraisals through Langs, you can contact:

Bob Langs
31R Turtle Cove
Raymond, Maine 04071
(207) 655-4265

IDENTIFYING COLLECTIBLES

The identification of fly fishing collectibles may be simple or difficult. Early, early collectible reels for instance may be difficult to identify if the reels are sporadic issues of individuals who did not produce in quantity, therefore did not sign or identify their pieces. These were few and far between, for many of the artisans of the day usually engraved the reels without their names and every so often identifying model numbers. Historians and collectors through the years have, with extensive research, been able to pinpoint some reels that would otherwise have remained unknown.

From the early 1800s reels were signed by their makers by means of engraving, which gave way almost uniformly to stamping around the mid 1800s.

Prior to the Civil War, most of the metalwork on reels consisted of brass and brass fasteners. Many early reels were unmarked up to the late 1800s but a great many were signed or scripted by their makers or engravers. Some of the older reels will have presentation inscriptions and engraved decor. The later and better old reels were fabricated or machined from German silver, and some were constructed of nickel silver and hard rubber compounds such as the Vom Hofe offerings. All Vom Hofe reels are clearly identified, marked, and labeled.

Most reels are easily identified by their logos, company stampings, and some will have dates and numbers.

George Snyder's business proliferated—early brass reels that were all quadruple multipliers incorporating jeweled pivots and steel gears. Early models had the pillar ends riveted to the baseplates. Milam and Hardman later improved upon the design utilizing screw assembly and repair. Meek reels after 1840 had screws and screw access holes with matching numbers, another identifying factor with Meek reels but not a critical one as all the Meek reels were signed and numbered.

The reels of the mid to late 1800s are the most

valuable and considered the rarest of known fly fishing collectibles.

Rods were usually signed by their makers or by the craftsmen who produced the rods for various companies. In some cases you will note a manufacturer emblem or logo on the rod prefixed or followed by the name of the rod crafter. The section on rods shows some typical examples. One sure method of distinguishing and identifying unknown or unsigned pieces is by studying the pages and illustrations of the various books dealing with fly fishing collectibles.

By far the most difficult fly collectibles to identify are flies themselves for there is no place on the fly where one can sign one's name or make a mark. Then, too, one fly by one flytier can be a dead ringer to a fly tied by another individual. Signed box sets by known flytiers or presentations sets with signed documentation provide a reliable method of matching flies to their origin. Flies that are mint in their original packaging are self-identifying and hence more valued than loose flies of undetermined origin.

Old creels are also hard to identify as many of

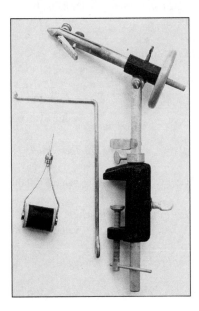

Some fly tying vises also rate as collectibles. This forty-year-old offering from Roto-vise of Holyoke, Massachusetts, was an early rotating version machined from aluminum.

the very old pieces have no identification attached. Here again one must play it by ear or trace the piece in an auction catalog or fly fishing collectible book.

For the most part, fly fishing collectibles, especially rods and reels, are easily identifiable as to producer or marker by stampings, engravings, or craftsmen's signatures.

FLY FISHING BOOK COLLECTIBLES

The Dry Fly Mans Handbook—Frederick Hanford
Routledge & Sons, London, 1913   value $100.00

Atlantic Salmon Flies & Fishing—Joe Bates
Stackpole, 1970 (First Edition)   value $100.00

Streamer Fly Tying & Fishing—Joe D. Baits, Jr.
Stackpole, 1970 (First Edition)   value $100.00

A Primer of Fly Fishing—Roderick Haig-Brown
William Collins, Toronto, 1964   value $50.00

Fishing the Dry Fly as a Living Insect—Joe D. Baits, Jr.
E.P. Dutton, N.Y., 1972   value $100.00

The Book of the Fly Rod—Sheringham and Moore
Mifflin Co., 1931   value $100.00

A Fly Fisher's Life—Charles Ritz
Crown, N.Y., 1972   value $100.00

The Way of a Trout with a Fly and Further Studies—
G.E.M. Skues
Black, London, 1921   value $200.00

The Salmon & Dry Fly—George La Branche
Houghton, Boston, 1924   value $200.00

Lee Wulff's Handbook of Freshwater Fly Fishing—
Lee Wulff
1939, First Printing   value $100.00

$\mathcal{E}$XHIBITING
AND STORING
FLY FISHING
COLLECTIBLES

Most collectibles are treasures and as such should be treated as display only items, though many collectors choose to use their pieces for casual if not intensive fishing. Rods, if well constructed, and reels will be protected against harm from use if they are treated with care. Reels should be cleaned and oiled regularly if used and not just thrown into a tackle box.

Smaller pieces can be stored in drawstring bags, boxes, or drawers but there are better means of storing and displaying. The best alternative methods are those that allow you to display your collection while keeping it secure and dust free.

Valued fly rods are best displayed or stored in special rod racks specifically designed to hold rods. These can be wood-faced, glass-enclosed, mounted on special grooves or dowel clamps, wood-backed, velvet-backed, whatever. If there are no budgetary restrictions you can have special racks or enclosures made to order by a qualified carpenter or wood finishing expert.

Rods can be mounted against a wall or within an enclosure by means of snap clips. Two to four clips for each rod will usually do the trick and the rods or rod segments can be slipped in and out of the clips with ease.

A visit to your tackle shop or boat dealer will yield a host of accessory rod mounts or rod mount fittings specifically designed for mounting and securing rods. Some alternatives are so fashionable and aesthetically attractive that they will add to or enhance the showroom's decor. Some commercial units will mount up to a dozen rods; double the amount if you want to place two rods to a slot.

Plastic or metal wall hooks available at most hardware or building supply outlets will allow you to wall-mount your rods horizontally, a neat alternative to the vertical method. This method is not only visually effective, but will allow you to mount a fair amount of rods in, say, a nine-foot-wide area.

Reels can also be displayed in a wide variety of ways. You can place them on bookshelves or you can have horizontal or vertical slatted racks, placing the reels in line on each small cubby segment. The best alternative method for reels is in glass-front-shelved enclosures or open-front plastic cubicles about three by four feet in size. Shelving can be ornate or finished wood (about ½" thick) and the back of the rack or enclosure can be mirrored so one can study both sides of the reel. Glass-enclosed racks can also be locked for security or to inhibit onlookers from handling the items.

Flies, streamers, bass bugs, and other tied artificials are best displayed on cork bulletin boards or cork-backed enclosures. The rear cork backing can also be faced in velvet or felt for aesthetic presentation. The cork boards can be custom framed or built up around the edges, then glass framed. Access can be through a hinged front glass and frame panel or through the rear for even more security. Flies can be pinned to the cork or soft backing material using the hook tips themselves. Under no circumstances should fly lures be used because even one fish strike can destroy a collectible fly.

For security and record purposes, don't neglect to inventory and categorize your personal collection. An index file such as a Rolodex or card and box file or even a simple notebook is essential for qualifying individual pieces as to their origin or manufacturer, commercial name or number, price value, and purchase price of the collectible item.

If you value your collection and its cost and have acquired some expensive pieces, consider insuring your collection or make sure there is a clause in your homeowner's policy that will protect your investment in case of fire or theft. In many instances your valued pieces come under the "antique" category, making them eligible for special insurance coverage. Make sure to photograph each valued item for identification and insurance verification. Keep notes on each single piece, its identifiable personal characteristics, unusual scratches or signs of wear, or even modification or repair regarding the item.

CHAPTER 8

HIGHLY RECOMMENDED READING

A Treasury of Reels, **Jim Brown**

This is undoubtedly the finest compilation on reels and their history, done under the auspices of the American Museum of Fly Fishing of Manchester, Vermont.

The book features the most comprehensive and accurate essay on the history of the fly reel, tracing its origin and development. One hundred fifty or so examples of reels from the museum's collection are illustrated and elaborated upon with superlative photography by Bob O'Shaugnessy and historical engravings and linecuts from old catalogs.

Unfortunately, the book is out of print but it is well worth tracing down in a used bookstore. The book itself is a collectible item. A true masterpiece no collector or historian should be without. Published in 1990 by the American Museum of Fly Fishing.

The Lawsons Guides, **George S. Lawson, Monteray Bay Publishing Co.**

The Lawsons guides are the definitive price guides to all fishing collectibles and a must for all collectors.

*The definitive book on reels issued by the American Museum
of Fly Fishing, out of print and now a collectible.*

*The Lawson
Guides are a must
for collectors.*

Lawsons Price Guide to Old Fishing Reels was
released in 1995 and features all the reels produced
since the inception of the commercial reel. There
are well over 5,000 listings in this manual arranged
by brand and model. Conditions and current values

are also defined and described. The book also defines in detail the grading systems that apply to collectible reels.

The new 1997 edition of *Lawsons Guide to Old Rods and Miscellaneous Tackle*, with over 2,500 listings of rods, including all old and valued fly rods, has just been released and a real asset it is to the collector. Special sections include: tackle boxes, licenses, and a host of other miscellaneous collectibles.

The 1996 edition of *Lawsons Price Guide to Old Fishing Lures* is also an essential book to the collector. This manual lists over 4,000 lures arranged by brand names and descriptions, color schemes, condition, and current collectible value.

Each of the Lawson manuals may be ordered by mail by sending a $19 check or money order plus $2.75 shipping and handling (for each book) to:

> Monteray Bay Publishing
> P.O. Box 796 (97-1)
> Capitola, California 95010

Handcrafting a Graphite Fly Rod, L.A. Garcia, Frank Amato Publications, Portland, Oregon

An interesting book in that it gives an insight into the makeup and production of a graphite fly rod. Garcia is an excellent rod maker and his personal rods, handcrafted, are sure to become collectibles in the future, as this book will be. The book is currently available through franchised bookstores or from the publisher:

> Frank Amato Publications
> P.O. Box 82112
> Portland, Oregon 97282
> (503) 653-8108

Old Fishing Lures and Tackle, Carl Freeman Luckey, Books Americana, Florence, Alabama

Luckey is the foremost expert on fishing collectibles, and he has compiled a virtual bible on the field of angling collectibles. His book is profusely illustrated and his technical orientation is right on. Some of the original patent illustrations throughout the book are both enlightening and interesting. An excellent documentation and a must for every serious collector. This volume is easily obtained through better franchised bookstores and is priced under $25, a great value.

Fly Tying, Helen Shaw, Ronald Press, New York

You will really be lucky if you can get your hands on this superb out-of-print book, originally released in 1963. And it will cost you some as it is a collectible item.

Helen Shaw was one of the greatest flytiers of all time, and her flies are extremely valuable and sought after by collectors who acknowledge her as a legendary figure. She was an honored member of the Fishing Hall of Fame and has received honors from the Sportsmen Club of America for being one of the world's greatest flytiers.

Two rare collectible books, excellent treatises on esoteric fly tying are: Vince Marinaro's Modern Dry Fly Code *and the great Helen Shaw's* Fly Tying.

Her classic book defines the rudiments of fly tying, and takes the reader step by step, in a most exacting manner, teaching how various fly styles are created. Probably the best, if dated, treatise on fly tying.

Collecting Old Fishing Tackle, John Muma
National Child Publishing Co.,
Lubbock, Texas

A nice soft-cover version is available and recommended for collectors and is crammed full of data and information essential to both the beginning and veteran collector.

The Collector's Guide to Antique Fishing Gear,
Silvio Calabi, Wellfleet Press

This book, too, gives the reader a wealth of information, particularly in reference to fishing antiques.

This book is available from:

> Book Sales Inc.
> 110 Enterprise Ave.
> Secaucus, New Jersey 07094

RECOMMENDED REFERENCE MATERIAL

Select Bibliography

The following books are specifically for collectors of old tackle. Some may be out of print but stocked in larger libraries.

American Sporting Collector's Handbook, New Revised Edition by Allan J. Liu. Copyright 1982, Winchester Press, P.O. Box 1260, Tulsa, Oklahoma 74101.

Esquire's Book of Fishing, Robert Scharff. Copyright 1933, Harper and Row, New York.

Field and Stream Treasury, Greg and McCluskey. Copyright 1955, Henry Holt and Company, New York.

Fishing in America, Charles F. Waterman. Copyright 1975, Holt, Rhinehart and Winston, New York.

Fishing and Collecting Old Reel and Tackle and History, Albert J. Munger, 2235 Ritter Street, Philadelphia, Pennsylvania 19125.

Fishing Tackle, a Collector's Guide by Graham Turner.

Great Fishing Tackle Catalogs of the Golden Age, Samuel Melner, Herman Kessler. Copyright 1972. Crown Publishers, Inc., New York.

Henry Loftie, Fly Fisherman, Inventor, Tackle Maker. Copyright 1987 by Richard R. Metcalf, 112 Sutton Drive, Syracuse, New York 13219.

VIDEOTAPES

Clyde Harbin: available in VHS from the following: Antique Lures-VHS Tapes, P.O. Box 154087, Irving, Texas 75015. Telephone: 1-800-634-8917.

Volume 1
   Antiques and Collectibles: An Overview
Volume 6
   1903-1916 Heddon Catalogs

SOURCES FOR OLD BOOKS AND MAGAZINES

Kenneth Anderson-Books
38 Silver Street
Auburn, Massachusetts 01501

Judith Bowman Books
Pound Ridge Road
Bedford, New York 10506

James Cummings-Bookseller
859 Lexington Avenue
New York, New York 10021

Gary L. Esterbrook-Books
P.O. Box 61453
Vancouver, Washington 98666

Hampton Books
Rt. 1, Box 202
Newberry, South Carolina 29108

Henderson and Park
500 Main
Greenwood, Missouri 64030

Melvin Marcher
6204 North Vermont
Oklahoma City, Oklahoma 73112

MANUFACTURERS OF FLY FISHING TACKLE

Though many of the historic fly fishing craftsmen and manufacturers have faded into history, there are still a few of the ol' timers around. Some still fly their initial colors; some have merged or have been bought out. The manufacturers of today are a handful in comparison to the wide ranks of yesteryear and it is the ol' timers or the survivors who have given us knowledge and have created the tackle industry by experimenting and progressing to the state-of-the-art equipment we enjoy today.

Following is a listing past and present of individuals, craftsmen, small businesses, and large corporations which have specialized in or sell and promote fishing tackle.

Present:

Abercrombie & Fitch
New York, N.Y.

Bronson Reel Co.
145 State Street
Bronson, Mich.

Chicago Tackle Co.
2752 W. Windsor
Chicago, Ill.

Gladding (South Bend)
5985 Tarbell Road
Syracuse, N.Y. 13217

Horrocks-Ibbotson Co.
Rome, N.Y.
Utica, N.Y.

W.J. Jamison
736 South California Avenue
Chicago, Ill.

Martin Reel Co.
30 East Main Street
Mohawk, N.Y.

Pflueger Sporting Goods
1801 Main Street
Columbia, S.C. 29202

Shakespeare Co.
3801 Westmore Drive
Columbia, S.C. 29204

Winchester Arms Co.
New Haven, Conn.

Past:

Thomas H. Bate & Co.
7 Warren Street
New York, N.Y.

Thomas H. Chubb
Post Mills, Vt.

Thomas J. Conroy
28 John Street
New York, N.Y.

James Heddon & Sons
414 West Street
Dowagiac, Mich. 49047

Hiram L. Leonard
Central Valley, N.Y.

William Mills & Son
Central Valley, N.Y.

Robert Ogilvy Co.
78 Chambers Street
New York, N.Y.

Perrine Mfg. Co.
704 South Fourth Street
Minneapolis, Minn.

Shapleigh Hardware
St. Louis, Mo.

Talbot Reel Co.
314-316 East 8th Street
Kansas City, Mo.

Fred E. Thomas
117 Exchange Street
Bangor, Maine

Edward Vom Hofe & Co.
112 Fulton Street
New York, N.Y.

Von Lengerke & Antoine
33 South Wabash Avenue
Chicago, Ill.

Von Lengerke & Detmold
349 Madison Avenue
New York, N.Y.

Yawman and Erbe
Rochester, N.Y.

INSTANT EXPERT QUIZ

1. Before American production began, fly rods were imported from what country?

2. What were the initial American fly rods fabricated from?

3. Who originated the first bamboo fly rod, and in what time period?

4. Of what was the first split bamboo fly rod composed?

5. How did Hiram Leonard improve upon the bamboo concept?

6. What was the earliest method of attaching reels to fly rods?

7. What fly reel concept originated at the onset of fly reel production and is still used and preferred today?

8. Flies tied today differ from flies of yesteryear in what respect?

9. What rod material offers the best action?

10. What fly rod materials are proving to be almost equal to bamboo and more durable as well?

11. Name the leading mass producers of fly rods?

CHAPTER 9

12. Degree of stiffness or curvature in a fly rod denotes its "action." Describe a quick action rod.

13. What is the major ingredient for the formation of fly reel handles?

14. What two cork materials are best suited and which is the most durable?

15. What is the most valuable collectible fly rod?

16. What was the forerunner of the true fly reel?

17. One of the earliest reels was of predominantly wood construction named after the city in England of its origin. What was this type of reel called?

18. Who in 1808 perfected a fly reel design for a 9x multiplying spool?

19. Who innovated the Sun and Planet reel style in the mid 1850s?

20. How much revenue on the collectible market will a pristine early Hardy Perfect reel generate?

21. Who invented that very rare collectible the "Bridge Reel?"

22. Who conceived the first successful raised pillar design reels?

Answers

1. England
2. Solid wood stock
3. Sam Philippi in the mid 1800s
4. Four strips of bamboo
5. He used six instead of four strips of bamboo
6. Cord, line, narrow cloth or leather over the reel foot securing the reel to a short segment at the bottom of the rod.
7. The single-action fly reel
8. Only in the choices of new plastic fibers, holographic materials, and fluorescent colors which can be used in place of older materials; in some cases more effective.
9. Split bamboo
10. Graphite and carbon fiber
11. Orvis, Pflueger, Penn, Cortland, Sage, Loomis and Fenwick
12. A quick action rod flexes and curves most in the upper quadrant of the rod.
13. Cork
14. Specie cork and mustard cork. Specie cork is the most durable.
15. A garrison 198—$8,000
16. The Birmingham reel
17. The Nottingham reel
18. T. Williamson
19. Peter Malloch
20. $5,000
21. William Billinghurst in 1859
22. Hiram Leonard

INDEX